KU-673-757

HarperCollins Publishers
Westerhill Road, Bishopbriggs Glasgow G642QT

First published 1996
This edition published 1999

Reprint 10 9 8 7 6 5 4

Created and produced by Flame Tree Publishing, part of The Foundry
Creative Media Co. Ltd, The Long House, Antrobus Road, Chiswick,
London W4 5HY

© The Foundry Creative Media Co. Ltd (text) 1996
© Natural Science Photographs (photographs) 1996 (except for those
listed on page 254)

ISBN 0 00 472276-0

Publisher's Note: Some pictures in this book show dogs with docked tails.
Docking is not recommended by the British Veterinary Association and is
now illegal unless performed by a qualified veterinary surgeon.

Special thanks to John Dunne

Printed in Italy by Amadeus S.p.A.

Contents

Introduction

Dogs are rightly regarded as the epitome of loyalty. Where else can one find refuge from the endless dissimulation, falsehood and treachery of humans, if not in dogs upon whose honest countenance one can gaze without mistrust.
Schopenhauer

Originally kept as hunters and workers, dogs have evolved in history to occupy a unique position in the human world, unparalleled by any other successfully domesticated animal. The pack instinct, the hunting

instinct, the protective instinct – each is a common ancestral trait which has enabled the development of a close and mutually beneficial relationship between dogs and their human owners since the earliest times.

The dog's willingness to become 'man's best friend' and to accept a human master as a substitute for a canine pack leader has allowed for its remarkably smooth integration into civilized society. A canine's ability to adapt is quite astounding when one pauses to consider how it has progressed from agrarian living to modern high-tech living without suffering the difficulties that have plagued so many other animal species. A dog will happily allow itself to be trained by man and remain unquestioningly loyal and submissive to the wishes of its master in return for shelter, companionship and an adequate standard of general care.

Over the centuries the dog's basic design has been altered dramatically either to fit in with man's working needs or to suit his preference for a certain canine temperament or physical feature. Nowadays, dogs come in a wide variety of shapes, sizes and colours and there is a breed to suit nearly every person's requirements.

It is hoped that this book will assist the ordinary dog-owner in their choice of canine companion as well as equipping them with all the essential information necessary to establish a highly rewarding and gratifying relationship with their dog.

How To Use This Book

This book details a wide variety of information about dogs – everything from facts about breeds, life-cycle and training, to famous dog names, nutrition and feeding, and classification. A series of photographs illustrates each topic.

The book is divided into eight sections, together with The Compendium at the end.

Each part is colour-coded for easy reference. Part One, which appears in green, presents general information about dogs, including their natural history, nature, anatomy and life-cycle. Part Two is colour-coded pink, and provides information about managing your dog – choosing and caring for your puppy, behaviour and training, and special information about training the older dog. Part Three discusses the Hound group and is coded blue. Part Four is coded yellow, with details about the Gundog group. Part Five, coded lilac, presents an in-depth discussion of the Terrier group. Part Six, coded deep green, introduces the Utility group. Part Seven, which is orange, is all about the Working group.

Parts Three to Seven provide all the essential information you will need to know about breeds around the world. You will find details of the breed's history and country of origin, and there is a breed basics box which presents practical details of the dog; for example, its size, pet suitability and uses.

The Compendium, coded blue, contains useful information about general aspects of dogs, from classification, breeding and showing, through to healthcare and famous dogs. There is also a handy list of addresses of various dog organizations, and a Glossary explaining terms which might be unfamiliar. At the end of the book you'll find an index which lists every subject and type of dog found in this book.

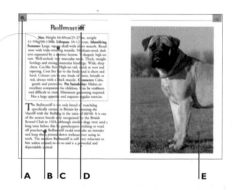

A The page number appears in a colour-coded box indicating which part you are in.

B Essential information about the breed appears in a concise and fascinating introductory passage.

C Breed basics list all the important details about a breed.

D The title of the chapter, in this case the breed name, appears at the beginning of every new section.

E The topic covered on this spread will be illustrated with clear photographs.

ALL ABOUT
❧ DOGS ❧

Natural History

The dog is part of a family of hunters and scavengers, including wolves, foxes, coyotes and jackals which are known as *Canidae*. All are carnivores with particularly long, narrow heads and jaws supplied with large, powerful, carnassial teeth. They have highly developed senses of sight, sound and smell.

• The earliest ancestor of the *Canids* appeared on earth 60 million years ago in the *Paleocene* epoch. Known as the *Miacis*, it was a weasel-like creature with the distinctive teeth of a carnivore which walked on the soles of its feet, unlike modern dogs which walk on their toes.

• Thirty million years later, during the *Oligocene epoch, Miacis* had evolved to become a primitive canid known as the *Cynodictis*.

• By the late *Miocene epoch*, ten to 15 million years ago, *Tomarctus* appeared, an animal with a long body and tail, social instincts similar to those of a dog.

• The first true *Canis* emerged between five and seven million years ago and had begun to walk on four of its toes. This creature eventually evolved to become an early wolf.

Descendants of this earliest form of wolf, living in various parts of the Northern Hemisphere, were the first to forge a bond with humans and were known as *Canis lupus Pallipes*. It remains uncertain when precisely this happened, but evidence suggests that some wolves altered their livestyles to live with humans in early villages about 10,000 years ago. Domestication did not simply occur overnight but co-operation between the two species arose after an aggregation of juvenile wolves in village dumps which then moved into the villages themselves to exploit waste. Man ate many of these, but also encouraged some for other uses, in particularly to guard, hunt and herd. Selecting for behaviour characteristics produced changes in physical appearance that lead to various types of dog which became shaped, many thousands of years later, into breeds, described primarily by how they look, rather than how they behave.

By the time man began to keep livestock, about 10,000 years ago, the dog was already domesticated enough to be used as a herding animal.

As farming communities began to spring up, it was more widely used to protect sheep and cattle against predators and to control vermin on the farms.

• Pictures of dogs painted on the walls of Egyptian tombs point to the fact that the people of ancient Egypt were one of the first to employ dogs for specific purposes, such as greyhounds to chase their prey.

• The ancient Greeks kept and developed a number of hound types and the Romans bred dogs from the earliest times, including greyhounds, bloodhounds and large mastiff types for hunting and warfare.

• Different types of dogs spread throughout Europe via trade routes, but were also scattered as a result of various military and political changes.

In medieval times hunting on horseback became an important leisure activity of the nobility leading to the development of more varieties of hunting dog, including special breeds of scent and sight hounds. The introduction of firearms was paralleled by the further development of specialist breeds to locate and retrieve game.

Countless generations of intensive breeding have resulted in a great diversity of dog breeds. There are now over 400 recognized breeds throughout the world and the numbers are increasing. The greatest impact on 20th-century breeds has been the creation of dog shows which have reduced the emphasis on a dog's usefulness in favour of its appearance.

Understanding Dogs

Many owners have a misguided perception of what a dog really is and entertain false expectations of their pet based on the assumption that a dog's level of

understanding is equal to their own. The speed at which a dog will co-ordinate information and organize in his mind an appropriate response, varies from breed to breed, but it is important to remember that dogs do not have the capacity to interpret complex human language, behaviour and emotions.

HOW INTELLIGENT IS A DOG?

• Dogs are capable of linking two ideas together, but do not link actions separated in time.

• If, for example, your puppy has made a mess on the floor prior to your arrival home from work, it is pointless to reprimand it for the misdeed.

• Dogs cannot understand our language. Sound patterns, intonation and facial and body language are far more important methods of communication.

• A dog is motivated by the desire to please and learning should be reinforced by reward so that an association is formed between a correct response and a pleasant aftermath.

NATURAL INSTINCTS

Although many of the wild, survival-orientated instincts of the dog have been suppressed through domestication, most dogs retain a territorial and predatory instinct to a varying degree.

• Natural pack behaviour will lead your dog to protect the home, which it considers the pack's communal den, against undesirable intruders. In most instances, a dog will look to its human owner, the pack leader, for instruction on how to behave towards a stranger.

• A dog will often have its own personal space within the communal territory and may want to defend its privacy. This might be a bed or a particular corner of the garden.

BEHAVIOURAL PROBLEMS

Sometimes, despite having chosen what we consider the correct dog to suit our needs and circumstances, problems may occur where the dog fails to integrate properly into the human family. This may be a result of its inadequate socialization as a young puppy, normal competitiveness or responses to anxiety. It is always better to prevent behavioural problems before they happen, than attempt to rectify them once they exist. Early training is advised for all dogs, although the extent to which it is necessary depends on the particular characteristics of the breed. Common problems to be avoided include nervousness, anxiety, possessiveness and anti-social behaviour, including aggression (see below).

AGGRESSION

A dog may display aggression in many different cirumstances; e.g., in its own self-defence, or to impose its will on other dogs or people.

Other common behavioural problems an owner may encounter include separation anxiety, inappropriate urination or defecation, phobias, or car and sheep chasing. Most can be cured in time, often with the help of a vet or a trained animal psychologist if the problem is a complex one. The important thing is to seek help early, intially from your vet and to ask for a referral to a member of the Association of Pet Behaviour Counsellors (APBC). Details of the APBC's many clinics nationwide can be obtained from the Secretary (see page 246).

General Anatomy

Dogs are powerfully built and resilient animals which have adapted extraordinarily well to the many changes they have undergone since living in the wild. All dogs share the same fairly primitive skeleton even though selective breeding has brought about many variations in external appearance.

SKELETON

• Three basic skull shapes exist. *Dolichocephalic*, which describes the elongated shape of breeds such as the Saluki; *mesocephalic*, which describes the medium-sized skull of a Pointer; and *brachycephalic*, found in short, snub-nosed breeds like the Pug.

• Spine and limb bones are tubular. Limbs are generally long and adapted for fast running.

- Bones of the skull, pelvis and shoulder blades are flat.
- Long ribs form a strong cage to protect the chest.
- Shoulder blades are detached from the rest of the skeleton allowing great freedom of movement when running.
- The spine is tube-shaped and made up of individual bones called *vertebrae* which continue into the tail. The *neural canal* housing the spinal cord runs through the centre of the spinal tube.
- The skeleton is held together by powerful ligaments, tendons and muscles. Ligaments secure bones to each other and permit controlled movement. Tendons are cords of tough tissue attaching muscles to bones. Dogs have three types of muscle: smooth, skeletal and cardiac.
- Muscles controlling leg movement are attached to the flat limb bones. The nervous system sends messages to these muscles causing them to alternately contract and relax so that the limb bones move.

THE BRAIN

• A dog's brain is much smaller than man's, in particular the *cerebrum* – the portion of the brain associated with intellectual function, emotion and personality.

• A large part of a dog's brain is occupied with sensory activity, particularly the interpretation of scent.

SIGHT

• The position of the eyes on a dog's head gives it a wider field of vision than humans'. Unless the eyes are situated at the front of the head the animal will tend to have poor stereoscopic vision and less ability to judge distance.

• Dogs have better eyesight in low light levels and are more sensitive to light than humans.

• Canines have three eyelids, an upper, a lower, and a third hidden under the lower lid protecting the eye from dirt and dust.

HEARING

• A dog's hearing is much sharper than man's and their ears are much more mobile.

• Dogs can detect high-frequency sounds inaudible to humans and have a greater sensitivity to sound than we do.

• Research has shown that a dog can pinpoint the source of a sound within six hundredths of a second.

SCENT

• Smell is the most highly developed sense in dogs. A dog has about 200 million scent receptors in its nose as opposed to humans who have 5 million.

• The region of a dog's brain which registers smell contains 40 times more cells than the equivalent area in a human brain.

• A dog's nose is moist in order to help it capture scent. Scents carried in the nasal secretions are passed to the nasal membranes which are lined with sensory cells leading directly to the olfactory bulb of the brain.

TASTE

• Dogs have fewer tastebuds than humans, 2000 compared to our 10,000.

• A dog's oesophagus has a thick lining which allows it to swallow large, solid food.

SKIN AND COAT

• Like a human, a dog's skin is made up of two basic layers, the epidermis and the dermis. The upper epidermis is not as robust as man's since the dog's coat assists in protecting the skin surface.

• Hair follicles, far more numerous in a dog than in a human, are embedded in the dermis, together with blood vessels and numerous skin glands, including the sebaceous glands, which lubricate the hair follicles.

• Except for a few hairless varieties, nearly all dogs are covered with a thick outer coat made up of hundreds of thousands of individual hairs known as guard hairs. These may or may not be surrounded by secondary hairs which produce a softer, woolier undercoat.

Life-Cycle

As with any other species of animal, courtship, mating and birth are the route to dogs' survival.

• Medium-sized and smaller breeds, and mongrels, tend to survive longer than giant ones. The average lifespan of a Great Dane, for example, can be as short as seven or eight years. A terrier, on the other hand, may outlive this larger relative by up to ten years.

• The smaller the breed, the smaller the litter. Toy dogs may only give birth to one or two pups and suffer considerable difficulties at birth. Giant breeds may have up to 14 pups in a litter.

• Animal scientists believe that a dog inherits 50 per cent of its inherited characteristics from the sire and 50 per cent from the dam.

REPRODUCTIVE SYSTEMS

• The reproductive systems of male and female dogs are not unlike those of humans. In the female, the sexual organs are located internally. The opening to the vagina, the vulva, is clearly visible below the anus. The uterus, or womb, are flanked by the fallopian tubes and the ovaries which release eggs for fertilization by the male sperm. In males, the penis and scrotum hang behind the hind legs.

• Although it varies from breed to breed, a male dog normally reaches sexual maturity at about ten months and is sexually active all year round, picking up the scent given off by any female in season.

• A bitch usually comes into 'heat' for the first time when she is between six and 12 months of age. This 'heat' period lasts for about three weeks, twice a year.

COURTSHIP AND MATING

• When the bitch is ready for mating, the vulva begins to swell and a discharge may be seen.

• Two to three days afterwards, the female willingly accepts a mate and holds her tail to one side. Usually she will accept several different mates to increase the likelihood of conception.

• Actual mating, when the male sperm is released, may last less than a minute. The dog mounts the bitch, clasping her body with his forelegs.

• Ejaculation may be followed by a period known as 'the tie'. While still joined, the male dismounts, draws a hindleg over the female's back, and turns around to stand with its back to the bitch.

• This period may last for up to half an hour and should be allowed to end naturally, although it is not considered necessary for conception.

• Even if your bitch is not pregnant, the body may begin to produce progesterone in preparation for birth. Your vet will usually be able to tell between 24 and 32 days after mating whether or not it is a false pregnancy.

BIRTH

• Bitches prefer a warm, dark, isolated place in which to give birth. As the time for whelping draws near, the bitch's temperature can drop to about 36 degrees C and the dog will appear out of sorts.

• Most bitches will refuse food 24 hours beforehand.

• Most females give birth lying down on their side. Each puppy is covered with a thin foetal membrane when delivered which the mother licks away vigorously thereby stimulating breathing in the newborn pup.

• Although most puppies are born head-first, a substantial number, sometimes as much as 40 per cent, may be born breach.

• The mother will chew away the umbilical cord from each pup and eat the afterbirth herself.

• Subsequent puppies may be born up to two hours after the first, but you may wish to consult your vet if the interval between pups exceeds this. You should always have your vet's emergency telephone number to hand during delivery.

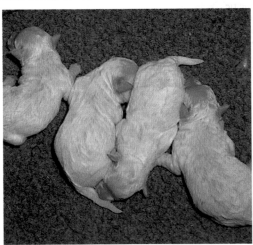

NEWBORN PUPPIES

• Puppies are born with their eyes shut and ears closed, but their sense of smell is acute enabling them to locate their mother's milk.

• The eyes start to open between ten and 14 days and the puppies are usually able to focus properly about a week after that.

• At birth, the ears are folded and the ear canals are sealed off. A newborn pup will begin to hear after about twelve days.

• Puppies normally feed from the mother until they are about four or five weeks old. Solid foods of a sloppy consistency should then be introduced gradually. Most puppies are weaned by about seven weeks.

• A puppy will usually begin to walk after three weeks.

• Newborn pups are unable to control their own body temperature and can suffer from hypothermia. The whelping box should be kept warm using an infrared lamp or electric blanket.

• A puppy begins socialization at about four weeks of age, when it learns to play and act as a member of the pack.

A QUICK GUIDE TO YOUR DOG'S AGE*

Dog	Human	Dog	Human
6 months	10 years	7 years	44 years
1 year	15 years	8 years	48 years
2 years	24 years	9 years	52 years
3 years	28 years	10 years	56 years
4 years	32 years	12 years	64 years
5 years	36 years	14 years	72 years
6 years	40 years	16 years	81 years

* This is an abridged version of a chart first published in *Dogs Today* magazine.

DOG
~ MANAGEMENT ~

Choosing the Right Puppy

Dog ownership calls for commitment and a responsible attitude. It should never be entered into on a casual basis. It is important to

acknowledge from the outset that your dog needs to be properly cared for by you and that it will prove itself a loyal and rewarding companion only if you are prepared to give enough in return. Before you even consider purchasing a dog, therefore, it is essential that you ask yourself a number of pertinent questions. If you can answer yes to all of them, then it is time to move on and decide what breed would best suit you.

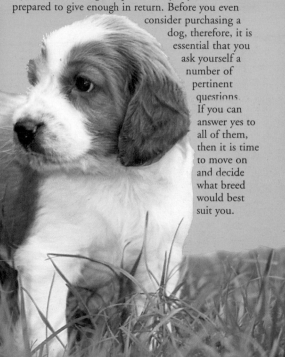

CONSIDERING A NEW ADDITION
TO THE FAMILY?

• Are you prepared to take responsibility for the well-being of your dog for a period of up to 14 years?
• Are you sure that the novelty value of owning a cute-faced puppy has not prompted your purchase?
• Can you afford to spend £3-5 per week on dog food, as well as extra sums on veterinary bills and insurance?
• Will you devote adequate time to training, exercising and grooming?
• Is your home large enough to accommodate your pet?
• Have you thought about introducing a new dog to a household with children?
• Will there be someone at home during the day to keep your dog company?
• Will somebody responsible look after your dog when you go on holiday?

Selecting the pet that suits your circumstances is very often a difficult task since there are hundreds of pedigree dogs to choose from as well as a huge variety of mongrels and crossbreeds. Decide first of all whether you want a male or a female. The cost of neutering bitches ought to be considered given the fact that they come into season about twice a year attracting a large number of male admirers. The following is a list of guidelines on how to choose and where to look:

PEDIGREE PUPPIES

• Visit a reputable breeder. The British Kennel Club can provide a list of addresses.
• Ask to see the mother of the litter and avoid dealers who offer lots of different breeds for sale. Take plenty of time over your decision.
• Arrange for the puppy to be seen by a vet soon after your purchase.
• Ask whether the breeder has registered the puppy and arrange for it to be returned if it proves to be unwell.

ADULT PEDIGREES

• Find out why the dog is being sold and how old it is.
• Try to assess its behaviour and general character in its home environment.

MONGRELS AND CROSSBREEDS

- Avoid purchasing from pet shops, try your local Rescue Centre instead.
- A friend or local vet is also a good source.
- The British Kennel Club can provide you with a list of centres with dogs and puppies, both pedigree and crossbreeds, needing good homes.
- Remember that the temperament of an adult dog will be less predictable and training may prove difficult.
- Be sensible and do not choose a dog because you like its appearance or feel sorry for it. It may soon lose its charm.

Caring For Your Dog

The majority of dogs do not have complicated needs, but all have certain simple requirements which ought to be met if your pet is to remain a fit and happy member of your household. To begin with, some basic equipment is necessary in order for your dog to settle into its new home more readily.

ESSENTIAL PROVISIONS

• All dogs require a clean and comfortable bed away from draughts. There is a whole range to choose from, including wicker-baskets, bean-bags, metal crates and plastic baskets. Even a large cardboard box lined with a blanket is perfectly acceptable if replaced from time to time.

• Your dog will need a food and water bowl.

• A collar and name-tag should be provided, together with a strong lead for exercising. These can be either leather or nylon. A potentially aggressive dog may require a muzzle when taken outdoors.

• All breeds will need a brush or a comb for grooming.

• A few safe, well-made toys will keep your dog occupied and encourage healthy gums as it chews on them.

GROOMING

Some grooming is necessary for whatever type of dog you choose and a regular routine should be established when the dog is very young. Try to make these occasions as pleasant as possible. This is an opportunity to show your dog who is in control, but it should also be a relaxing and enjoyable experience, and should never be associated with discomfort or fear.

• Basic grooming, apart from brushing and combing, may also involve nail-clipping, ear, eye and teeth-cleaning, bathing, cutting and stripping the coat.

• Your equipment should include a suitable brush and comb, nail-cutters, scissors, cotton wool, toothbrush and canine toothpaste. Heavy tartar should be removed by your veterinary surgeon.

• When bathing your dog use a dog shampoo, as human shampoos may contain irritants. Always put cotton wool in your dog's ears to protect them and make sure the coat is rinsed thoroughly.

• A dog's anal glands, situated underneath the tail, will need emptying from time to time. The liquid gathered may lead to an abcess if it is not removed. Your vet will do this for you.

EXERCISE

Most healthy dogs enjoy taking excercise and it is essential for all breeds to do so whether large or small. Most dogs get far less exercise than they need which often leads to destructive behaviour.

• All dogs require at least 30 minutes' free-running exercise per day.

- Make exercise fun by introducing toys such as frisbees or rubber balls and allow the dog to retrieve them for you.
- Swimming is excellent exercise, but never force your dog into the water. Some of the more athletic breeds also enjoy running alongside a bicycle on a traffic-free road.
- Research suggests that many dog owners suffer less heart disease as a result of exercising their pets than those who do not have dogs.

Nutrition and Feeding

All dogs will be happier and healthier if fed a sensible, well-balanced diet that includes protein, carbohydrate, fatty acids, vitamins and minerals. Discovering what best suits your dog's tastebuds is often a case of trial and error and the task is not made any easier by the huge variety of manufactured pet-food of different textures and calorific content now readily available.

Many of these manufactured foods are complete foods, containing all the nutrients essential for your dog's well-being. Others need to be mixed with complementary feed. Obviously, the size and age of your dog will dictate

its nutritional requirements and you will need to calculate your dog's ideal calorie intake.

While most adult dogs will eat a wide range of foodstuffs similar to those contained in a human diet, including meat, vegetables, cereals and even fresh fruit, puppies need careful feeding up until the age of about seven months.

FEEDING YOUR PUPPY

• A puppy requires up to five small meals a day from the age of six weeks to six months and two meals a day thereafter.

• Food should include small amounts of raw or cooked chicken or red meat, green leafy vegetables and wholemeal biscuit. The meal should be moistened with milk or gravy. Special food is available for growing puppies.

• A drastic change of diet is not advisable; ask your breeder what the pup was being fed on before you acquired it.

• Introduce new foods gradually. Use bottled mineral water for the first few days until the pup is accustomed to your tap water.

GENERAL FEEDING TIPS

• Don't serve food straight from the refrigerator and never give a dog stale food, or meat that has been left sitting in a tin.

• A good supply of fresh drinking water should always be available.

• Bones are not essential for a healthy diet and you should certainly never feed your dog dry, brittle bones. A large, raw marrow bone is the best type for your dog, adding calcium to the diet as well as keeping teeth and gums healthy.

• Try not to feed your dog confectionery and other sweet snacks. Nutritious chews and biscuits are available should you need to reward your dog between meals.

Dog Behaviour and Training

All dogs have a unique temperament and the breed group to which they belong is only a general guide to likely inherited traits. Working dogs, for example, have a reputation for being quick to learn and very biddable but this varies from individual to individual. The behaviour of your dog directly reflects your ability to care for it properly. Dogs can be very sociable animals and rewarding companions if properly trained, but left to their own devices, they will quickly test the limits of acceptable behaviour.

Dogs are pack animals and their natural instinct is to follow the leader within that pack. The domestic dog is more than happy to join the human pack and to be governed by a human leader, but it is the owner's responsiblity to curb natural aggression and to socialize his charge. For a dog to become successfully integrated into the home, proper training from an early age is essential.

A puppy's socializing period begins when it is four weeks old and lasts until it is about 14 weeks old. During this important time, your dog should be exposed to as many different human experiences as possible. The more your puppy sees, hears, touches and tastes, the more it meets and plays with other dogs, children and adults, the better equipped it will be to cope with adult life. Research has proven that dogs which are not introduced to everyday activities early on, for example, walking alongside traffic, may grow fearful of such things and suffer behavioural problems later on.

Puppies are not normally innoculated until they are about eight weeks old, but this does not mean they must be isolated from the outside world. Caution is necessary, however. Take care not to put your puppy on the ground where other dogs have been. Carrying it, or taking it out with you in the car is a good compromise.

First Lessons For Your Puppy

The first thing to remember when your new puppy arrives at your home is that it is very much a baby, cut off from its mother and likely to be very unsettled and nervous as a result. It will need lots of reassurance and gentle encouragement to begin with. 'No' should not be the first word a puppy learns to understand and it should never be shouted at or physically punished for failing to live up to your expectations. Reward-based training is a far more humane and successful way of training your dog.

• Begin by teaching your puppy simple skills such as how to walk to heel, how to sit when commanded, how to stay or lie down. Always acknowledge obedience either with food treats, patting of the head or verbal praise. Be patient and your dog will eventually learn.

• Teach your puppy its name so that it comes to you every time it is called. Always use a friendly, reassuring tone and do not use the name in reprimand.

WALKING TO HEEL

• Shorten your dog's lead sufficiently for it to walk alongside you, its right shoulder at your left leg.

• Walk calmly forward in a straight line, repeating the word 'heel' in a firm tone of voice.

• Check from time to time that your dog is not falling behind or racing ahead.

TEACHING YOUR DOG TO SIT

• Choose a relatively quiet place, free from distractions to teach your dog to sit as soon as the art of walking to heel has been mastered.

• Put firm, yet gentle pressure on the dog's back, above the pelvis and repeat the word 'sit'.

• To begin with, you must speak this command in conjunction with the hand movement. Your dog will initially understand your words only if accompanied by a physical demonstration.

HOUSE-TRAINING

Often the puppy's life is made very miserable by its owners impatience to house-train it. Dogs have a natural instinct to keep their living area clean, but when nature calls and they do not have access to the outdoors, they will relieve themselves on the spot. It is important that this habit is broken early on, but your dog cannot do it alone.

• Take your puppy into the garden at regular intervals and stay with it until it has emptied either its bladder or bowels. Offer lots of praise when it has finished.

• Puppies will nearly always want to relieve themselves first thing in the morning, so always take them out at this time.

• Rubbing your dog's nose in its own mess will not solve the problem. Wait for the next opportunity when your puppy squats on the floor. Lift the puppy up firmly and carry it through to the garden.

Training and the Older Dog

It is not always possible for the owner to obedience train their dog from an early age. An older dog, for example, may have been acquired from a Rescue Centre with well-established habits that may prove difficult to undo. With perseverance, however, the older dog will adapt to its new environment and learn to respect you as a new authority.

• Older dogs will require a gentle approach and more patient training.

• It should never be necessary to raise your hand in anger.

• Reward good behaviour and progress with small treats of food.

• Seeking professional assistance is often an extremely good idea. Do not hesitate to enrol for weekly obedience-training classes. Veterinary clinics will offer advice or you can contact your local dog-training centre.

• Remember that an older dog will tire more easily than a puppy. A rigorous routine is not advisable.

• Behaviour problems may exist in an older dog and you may require a pet behaviour counsellor to give you advice on how to cope (see page 18).

• Training will make your dog feel secure, and he'll know his boundaries. An undisciplined dog of any age will feel confused.

THE
∾ HOUND GROUP ∾

Group Features

The Hound Group includes the various breeds which helped man to hunt for centuries all over the world. These dogs are roughly divided into two groups: those which hunt by sight, for example, the Afghan, Saluki or Greyhound; and those which hunt by

scent, for example, the Basset Hound or Bloodhound.

Sight hounds, one of the earliest groups to emerge, are clearly depicted in Egyptian tomb paintings and are also described in ancient Persian manuscripts. In their Middle Eastern birthplace they were bred selectively to chase, capture and kill prey in open country. These are silent hounds with keen eyesight, renowned for their sprinting ability. Their appearance is invariably lean and graceful.

• Sight hounds were probably introduced to Britain over 2500 years ago by Phoenician traders.

• Today, they still retain a strong tendency to chase, even though most are now kept as companions.

Scent hounds evolved much later than sight hounds and were very much a European invention. Medieval France was particularly keen to develop such hounds, and produced both griffons and bassets. Scent hounds are more heavily built and slower in action and were used to scent out prey and put it up for the chase. They are marathon runners rather than sprinters, expected to follow a scent trail and run the quarry until it is exhausted. Some scent hounds are allowed to kill their prey. Others are trained to keep it at bay and then 'give tongue' attracting the huntsman's attention.

• Scent hounds nearly always hunt in packs using the huntsman as pack leader.

• Their hearing is relatively unimportant during a chase and they will hunt methodically, nose to the ground.

Most of today's British and Continental hounds, in particular the Bloodhound, are believed to be descended from a pack of hounds produced by Saint Hubert in the Ardennes in the sixth century. A great many were first brought to England during the Norman Conquest.

Spitz breeds are generally considered northern territory dogs, but they are spread throughout the world and there is no evidence to suggest that they originated in any one particular region like the greyhounds. The existence of so many indigenous spitz breeds suggests that they are possibly the oldest type of domesticated dog.

Afghan

Size: Height 64-74cm/25-9ins, weight
23-27kg/50-60lb. **Lifespan:** 12-14 years.
Identifying Features: Long skull. Strong jaws, proud,
powerful neck. Well-muscled shoulders. Finely textured
coat. Can be any colour. **Character:** Dignified,
sensitive and aloof with a strong independent streak.
Pet Suitability: Has a powerful hunting instinct and
can be difficult to train. Not for cramped households.

The Afghan is a member of the greyhound family
which first made an appearance thousands of years
ago in countries bordering the eastern Mediterranean.
Bred for its acute vision and speed, this dog type
eventually reached Afghan via ancient trade routes,
proving itself an excellent herder and powerful hunter,
comfortable in the roughest terrain. For centuries it remained the Afghanistan royal family's most valued hunting companion.

Basenji

Size: Height 41-43cm/16-17ins, weight 9.5-11kg/21-24lb. **Lifespan:** 12 years. **Identifying Features:** Flat skull, tapering towards nose. Profusely wrinkled forehead. High-set tail, curving tightly in a ring over spine. Colour is pure black and white; red and white; black, tan and white. **Character:** Intelligent, independent and affectionate, sometimes aloof with strangers. **Pet Suitability:** Not an ideal domestic pet.

Dogs with characteristics like those of the Basenji, first appeared in mural paintings on the tomb walls of the ancient Egyptians. Victorian explorers discovered similar dogs in the Congo basin where they were used by their African owners to find game and drive it into traps. The Basenji cannot bark, although when provoked it will yelp rather like a wolf.

Basset Hound

> **Size:** Height 33-38cm/13-15ins, weight
> 18-27kg/40-60lb. **Lifespan:** 12 years.
> **Identifying Features:** Dome-shaped skull. Sunken,
> lozenge-shaped eyes. Excessively wrinkled skin. Colour
> is usually black, white and tan (tricolour); or lemon
> and white (bicolour). **Character:** Placid and
> affectionate. **Pet Suitability:** A warm, fun-loving dog,
> suited to both urban and rural life. Good with
> children, but sometimes obstinate.

The word 'basset' means dwarf in French and all the
Basset breeds originated in France where they were
first mentioned in the mid-16th century. This dog is
distinguished by its closeness to the ground and by its
impressive ability to pick up a scent. The Basset Hound
prefers to hunt in packs and enjoys outdoor life
immensely.

Basset Griffon Vendeen

Size: (Grand) Height 38-42cm/15-16ins, weight 18-20kg/40-44lb. (Petit) Height 34-38cm/13-15ins, weight 14-18kg/31-40lb. **Lifespan:** 12 years. **Identifying Features:** Elongated, domed skull. Large, dark eyes with fur on the eyebrows. Long ears hanging below the muzzle. Long, robust neck. Deep chest. Colours are generally white, orange and white or tricolour. The Grand may also be grey, black and white, or tan and white. **Character:** (Grand) Obstinate, but affectionate. (Petit) Alert and enthusiastic. **Pet Suitability:** Good with children and other dogs but needs a lot of physical exercise.

The Basset Griffon Vendeen comes in two sizes, 'grand' and 'petit'. Both breeds are a less exaggerated, hairy alternative to the standard Basset Hound. They do not share the same serious expression, or the same wrinkling of the skin and are more lightly built with a harsh, shaggy coat. The characteristics of both breeds were properly fixed in France in the 1940s.

Beagle

Size: Height 33-40cm/13-16ins, weight
8-14kg/18-30lb. **Lifespan:** 13 years.
Identifying Features: Slightly domed skull. Large, dark
eyes set well apart. Long ears with rounded tips.
Colour can be black, tan and white, or any mingling
of these three, but not liver. Tip of the tail is white.
Character: Friendly, tranquil and alert.
Pet Suitability: Not suited to urban life. Good with
children, but can be obstinate.

The Beagle is the smallest of the British scent
hounds whose ancestors may be traced to William
the Conqueror's arrival in Britain. The original beagles,
some measuring under 25cm (10ins), were known as
Pocket Beagles and were carried by hunters in their
saddlebags. The
larger beagle
which evolved
from this strain
was kept almost
entirely as a
working dog
until the 1940s.
Nowadays, it is
equally popular
as a pet.

Bloodhound

Size: Height 58-66cm/23-26ins, weight 36-50kg/80-110lb. **Lifespan:** 10-12 years. **Identifying Features:** Long, narrow skull with prominent occipital peak. Deep folds of skin on foreface, pendulous upper lips. Colour can be black and tan, liver and tan, and red. Occasionally small amount of white on chest, feet and tip of tail. **Character:** Sensitive and affectionate. **Pet Suitability:** Not suited to urban life. Good with children.

The Bloodhound is the largest of the scent hounds, possessing a unique nose and an extraordinary ability to track human beings. Today they are used by prison authorities in many parts of the world to track down escaped criminals. The Abbey of St Hubert,

founded in the Ardennes in AD687, is said to have bred Bloodhounds for deer hunting while, at the same time, almost identical hounds were being bred in Great Britain.

Borzoi

> **Size:** Height 69-79cm/27-31ins, weight
> 35-48kg/75-105lb. **Lifespan:** 11-13 years.
> **Identifying Features:** Long, lean head. Dark, oblong,
> close-set eyes. Small, pointed ears. All colours
> acceptable, often white with patches of red or black.
> **Character:** Sensitive, independent and often aloof.
> **Pet Suitability:** Not good with cats or children.
> Needs open spaces to exercise.

The Borzoi is a powerfully built sight hound of great agility and power. It was developed from the Persian greyhound in the 17th century when it was crossed with native sheepdogs to produce an animal that could withstand harsh Russian winters and protect its master from local wolves. Queen Victoria was presented with a Borzoi by the Tsar of Russia :they subsequently became fashionable companions.

Deerhound

Size: Height 71-76cm/28-30ins, weight 36-45kg/80-100lb. **Lifespan:** 11-12 years.
Identifying Features: Long, flat skull, tapering dramatically to the nose. Dark eyes with black rims. High-set ears. Strong jaws. Colours can be dark blue-grey, yellow, brindle, sandy-red or red-fawn.
Character: Gentle and friendly, seldom aggressive or nervous.
Pet Suitability: Easily trained and obedient. Needs open space and coat needs regular attention.

The Deerhound is another descendant of the greyhound, first introduced to Britain by Middle Eastern traders almost 3000 years ago. As it moved further into northern Europe it developed a tougher, wiry coat to cope with the colder weather. It was originally kept by Scottish chieftains for hunting, and ownership was restricted to the Scottish nobility.

Dachshund

Size: Height (Miniature and Standard)
13-25cm/5-10ins, weight (Miniature) 4.5kg/10lb,
(Standard) 6.5-11.5kg/15-25lb. **Lifespan:** 14-17 years.
Identifying Features: Long, tapering skull. Obliquely
set, almond-shaped eyes. High-set ears. Strong jaws
with very powerful teeth. Slightly arched neck,
without dewlap. Long, full muscled body. Very strong
forequarters and forelegs. Firm padded, full feet with
strong nails. Slightly curved tail following line of the
spine. Can be all colours, but white markings
undesirable. **Character:** Loyal, yet independent.
Pet Suitability: An intelligent and defiant dog,
not ideal for young families. Long-haired varieties
need regular grooming.

The Dachshund, whose name means 'badger dog', is
considered to be a German breed, although ancient
Mexican carvings and Egyptian sculptures depict similar
looking short-legged dogs. First introduced to Britain by
Queen Victoria's Germanic husband in the 19th
century, the Dachshund was widely used for hunting,
making full use of its elongated shape, stunted legs and
big feet to travel down holes and dig out its prey.

Six breeds of Dachshund exist today, descended
from the taller, more hound-like 19th century dog.
There is a miniature and standard variety of three types:
the Smooth-haired, the Long-haired and the
Wire-haired.

English Foxhound

> **Size:** Height 58-69cm/23-27ins, weight
> 25-34kg/55-75lb. **Lifespan:** 11 years.
> **Identifying Features:** Flat skull, long, square muzzle
> with large nostrils. Colour is bicolour or tricolour.
> **Character:** Affectionate. **Pet Suitability:** Far more
> suited to rural than urban life. Often difficult to train.
> Requires regular exercise.

The English Foxhound is a robust, working dog with a keen nose and a good voice. Originally created from English staghounds and various French hounds, it became a very popular breed with the surge in fox-hunting in the mid-18th century. Today, most English foxhounds retain a strong hunting instinct and make excellent sporting companions.

Finnish Spitz

Size: Height 39-50cm/15.5-20ins, weight
14-16kg/31-35lb. **Lifespan:** 12-14 years. **Identifying
Features:** Dark eyes with black rims. Black nose and
lips. Small, sharply pointed ears. Strong, straight
forequarters, powerful hind legs. Colour is usually
reddish-brown, or red-gold on back with lighter
shading. **Character:** Lively, friendly and independent.
Pet Suitability: Strong-willed, not suitable for
households with small children or other pets.

The purity of the Finnish Spitz breed was
threatened at the beginning
of this century in its native
Finland prompting the
government to draw up a
standard by which it should
be judged. It is now the
most popular dog in
Finland, recognized as the
national breed.
Also referred to as the
'Barking Bird Dog', it is
a keen hunter of game
birds, particularly
grouse.

Greyhound

Size: Height 69-76cm/27-30ins, weight 27-32kg/60-70lb. **Lifespan:** 10-12 years. **Identifying Features:** Long, flat skull. Powerful, well-chiselled jaws. Long, straight forelegs and muscular hindquarters. Colour can be black, white, red, blue, fawn, fallow, brindle or any of these colours with white. **Character:** Gentle, even-tempered and affectionate. **Pet Suitability:** Good, relaxed housepets. Not good with cats. Need less exercise than people imagine.

The earliest images of greyhounds appear in the murals of ancient Egypt and in decorations on Greek and Roman pottery. These dogs probably reached England around 400 BC and ownership was at first restricted to landowners who made full use of their hunting instinct. By the 18th century, coursing was a popular sport. Greyhound racing originated in America during the early 20th century and the first dog track was opened in England in 1926. The greyhound has reached speeds of up to 60kmh/37mph.

Ibizan

Size: Height 56-74cm/22-29ins, weight 19-25kg/42-55lb. **Lifespan:** 12 years.
Identifying Features: Flat, elongated skull. Large, thin, mobile ears. Very lean, long, muscular neck. Straight legs and lean thighs. Smooth or wiry coat, hard and dense to the touch. Colour is white, chestnut, red, fawn or any combination of these.
Character: Dignified and intelligent. **Pet Suitability:** Not suited to an urban lifestyle. Independent and difficult to obedience train.

The Ibizan hound was brought to the Mediterranean thousands of years ago by traders and is now found on the island of Ibiza, as the name suggests, and also in parts of mainland Spain. In Mediterranean France,

where the breed also spread, it became known as the Charnique. It is a controlled and agile hunter, able to jump great heights without a take-off run.

Irish Wolfhound

Size: Height 71-90cm (28-35ins),
weight 40-55kg (90-120lb). **Lifespan:** 11 years.
Identifying Features: Long head with extended muzzle.
Dark, oval eyes with black eyelids. Colours can be
grey, brindle, red, black, pure white, fawn and wheaten.
Character: Patient and sensitive.
Pet Suitability: Very reliable with children and
other pets. Good watchdog. Demands a great deal of
open space and exercise.

The Irish Wolfhound is the largest breed of dog in the
world, probably transported to Ireland by Roman
armies. The early chieftains of Ireland kept these hounds
to protect them from wolves and to hunt boar and stag.
They flourished until the 16th century, but by the late
17th century they were almost extinct until Captain Graham, a British army officer revived the breed.

Norwegian Elkhound

Size: Height 49-52cm/19-21ins, weight 20-23kg/44-50lb. **Lifespan:** 12-13 years. **Identifying Features:** Wedge-shaped skull. Upstanding pointed ears. Strong and powerful legs. Comparatively small feet with protective hair between the thick pads. Always various shades of grey with black tips to outer coat. **Character:** Energetic, intelligent and independent. **Pet Suitability:** Good working dog with a powerful tracking instinct. Ideal for the country.

The Norweigan Elkhound is a typical member of the hardy spitz group, classified amongst hounds in Britain because it hunts by scent. The breed has existed in Scandinavia for approximately 5000 years and was originally bred for elk hunting, a task demanding a great

deal of power, concentration and stamina. It has a dense coat and sturdy frame, enabling its survival in the very cold climate.

Otterhound

Size: Height 58-67cm/23-27ins, weight 30-55kg/65-120lb. **Lifespan:** 12 years.
Identifying Features: Oval-shaped skull. Narrow, inward-folding ears covered with long hair, reaching to the end of the nose. Tightly padded feet with webbed toes. Colours are white with lemon, orange, tricolour or grizzle markings. **Character:** Amiable and even-tempered. **Pet Suitability:** Needs a very dedicated owner to provide adequate exercise and overall care.

Possibly descended from the Bloodhound, the Otterhound was bred exclusively for hunting outdoors, displaying a unique skill in tracking aquatic animals such as the otter. A thick, insulating undercoat allows the dog to swim safely in the most icy water. The hound's complete absorption in tracking a scent makes it deaf to all commands however, and it is not suitable for the average pet owner.

Pharaoh

Size: Height 56-63cm/22-25ins, weight
20-25kg/45-55lb. **Lifespan:** 12-14 years.
Identifying Features: Long, sculpted head. Intelligent,
amber eyes. Colour is tan with white markings on tip
of tail, chest and toes. Occasionally, a thin white blaze
on face. **Character:** Playful and alert.
Pet Suitability: Not suited to urban life. Strong
hunting instinct makes it difficult to train.

One of the oldest breeds of dogs in the world,
the Pharaoh has altered little in appearance over
5000 years. Similar dogs were painted on the walls of
the pyramids and this breed particularly resembles
the Egyptian dog-headed deity, Anubis. Pharaoh hounds

were brought
to Malta and
Greece by
Phoenician
traders
approximately
2000 years
ago and are
known as
rabbit dogs
in Malta.

Rhodesian Ridgeback

Size: Height 61-67cm/24-27ins, weight 30-39kg/65-85lb. **Lifespan:** 12 years. **Identifying Features:** Flat skull. High-set ears tapering to a rounded point. Coat is short, dense and sleek. Colour is light wheaten to red wheaten. **Character:** Dignified and reserved, never aggressive. **Pet Suitability:** Loyal companions and good guards. Suited to either urban or country life but needing lots of exercise. Not good with other dogs or small children.

Ancient strains of the Rhodesian Ridgeback were used to protect flocks and herds from predators. With the arrival of European settlers in Africa, inter-breeding occurred and the improved breeds were expected to guard lonely farms and to hunt big game. They were used in 'lion country' to track lions, taunting them and holding their attention until the animals were shot.

The Rhodesian Ridgeback is distinguished by a peculiar ridge of hair running down the spine in the opposite direction to the rest of its coat.

Saluki

Size: Height 58-71cm/23-28ins, weight 14-25kg/31-55lb. **Lifespan:** 12 years.
Identifying Features: Long, narrow skull. Deep-set dark eyes. Long ears covered with silky hair. Supple, well-muscled neck. Colours can be white, cream, fawn, golden red, grizzle, silver grizzle, tricolour (white, black and tan), or black and tan. **Character:** Dignified and independent. **Pet Suitability:** Affectionate with children, but not ideal with cats. Needs room to exercise freely. Requires regular grooming.

Also nicknamed the Gazelle Hound, the Saluki originated in the Middle East where it was highly prized by its Arab masters and could only be passed on as a gift. Although most Muslims regarded dogs as unclean, the Saluki was allowed to share tents with its nomadic masters and became an invaluable desert hunting companion.

Segugio Italiano

Size: Height 52-58cm/20.5-23ins, weight
18-28kg/40-62lb. **Lifespan:** 12-13 years. **Identifying
Features:** Large, dark eyes. Low-set, triangular ears
reaching to tip of nose. Oval feet with black nails.
Short, dense, glossy coat. Colour is fawn or black and
tan. **Character:** Affectionate and even-tempered.
Pet Suitability: Equally good as a working dog and
companion. Minimum grooming required.

The Segugio is a
versatile hunting
dog, capable of great
speed and endurance
in the field. Its
ancestry may well
reach as far back as
ancient Egyptian
coursing hounds.
Nowadays the
breed's stamina has
been improved with
the introduction of
mastiff blood. It is Italy's
only native scent hound and
it is highly regarded as a
hunter, mostly of hare, with a
truly exceptional nose.

Whippet

> **Size:** Height 47-51cm/18.5-20ins, weight
> 12.5-13.5kg/27-30lb. **Lifespan:** 13-14 years.
> **Identifying Features:** Long, tapering skull.
> Oval-shaped, alert eyes. Fine, short coat. Can be any
> colour. **Character:** Affectionate and even-tempered.
> **Pet Suitability:** Highly adaptable and easy to train.
> Suited to both domestic and sporting surroundings.
> Good with children and other pets.

The Whippet has only been in Britain for about 100 years. It may have been the result of cross-breeding between Italian Greyhounds and various terriers or it could have evolved from inter-breeding between Pharaoh Hounds and Maltese Rabbit Dogs brought to

Europe by the Romans. The Whippet can run and hunt with impressive speed, reaching speeds of up to 65kmh/40mph over short distances.

THE GUNDOG GROUP

Group Features

- Gundogs, including pointers, setters, retrievers and spaniels, have only been in use since the invention of firearms.
- Hunting, pointing, and retrieving game are the main duties of these dogs.

• They are usually highly intelligent and loyal dogs needing lots of stimulation.

• Today they are used for flushing, finding and retrieving game birds, but they also respond extremely well to training and make excellent service dogs.

The gundog is not allowed to catch or chase its quarry. It scents the air for the birds and then crouches low to the ground remaining immobile and silent until the bird's location is made known to the hunter. The dog is expected to stop dead in its tracks, watching its master shoot the target, before going to retrieve the dead or wounded prey. A 'soft mouth' ensures that the dog does not damage the target with its teeth. Unlike the

Greyhound, which will chase without restraint once released into the field, the gun dog must hunt energetically but also exercise a great deal of self-control. This is only possible with careful and early training.

Gundogs can be divided into various kinds, used for different jobs in the shooting field. Some breeds are good all-rounders, for example the Weimaraner, others are expert at one skill and work together with a number of dogs in the field.

• Some gundogs have sensitive noses and are used to flush out the game.

• Others point or set.

• A third group will retrieve game after it has been shot.

• Dogs such as the Irish Spaniel or Curly-Coated Retriever are good examples of water-loving gundogs.

There are now quite a number of gundogs to choose from depending on the needs of the sportsman. The large and versatile English Springer Spaniel is probably best suited to rough shooting. Pointers and setters need open space where they can range out and find the game. Labradors and Golden Retrievers are eager to learn and obey and possess a particularly gentle mouth.

• Gundogs are usually easier to train than other groups, and are suitable pets as well as working dogs.

• Gundogs are one of the most popular companion dogs, despite their reputation for superb hunting skills.

Brittany

Size: Height 46-52cm/18-20.5ins, weight 13-15kg/28-33lb. **Lifespan:** 13-14 years. **Identifying Features:** Coat is flat, dense and slightly wavy. Colour can be orange and white, liver and white, black and white or roan, or tricolour. **Character:** Affectionate, workmanlike and eager to please.
Pet Suitability: Good companion as well as being a good working dog. Easy to train, good with children.

The Brittany Spaniel, the most popular native breed in France, is a very attractive, medium-sized dog, often described as a spaniel, but very much a pointer in function and nature. It is thought to be a cross between British hunting dogs and the local Breton spaniel type, and is capable of hunting, pointing and retrieving. It is very obviously faster than other spaniel breeds and is still very rare in Britain.

English Setter

Size: Height 61-69cm/24-27ins, weight 25-30kg/55-66lb. **Lifespan:** 14 years.
Identifying Features: Long, silky, slightly wavy coat with feathering along chest and forelegs. Colour is black and white, liver and white, lemon and white or tricolour. **Character:** Very friendly and good-natured.
Pet Suitability: Good with children and other pets if trained early.

Probably descended from spaniels, the English Setter appeared in Britain some time in the 13th century. Cross-breeding with the pointer took place later on and then in the 19th century the dogs were again improved by two English breeders, Sir Edward Laverack and Sir Purcell Llewellin. In Britain nowadays, the English Setter is no longer used as a gundog, but in the United States there are still two types – a working and a show ring variety.

Gordon Setter

Size: Height 62-66cm/24-26ins, weight
25-30kg/56-65lb. **Lifespan:** 13 years.
Identifying Features: Coat is flat and silky with
fringes on belly, chest and throat. Colour is deep
shining coal black with rich tan markings.
Character: Outgoing and even-tempered.
Pet Suitability: Good all-round companion, loyal and
obedient. Good with children and other dogs.

The old name for the Gordon Setter was the Black
and Tan setter, a breed first mentioned as far back
as 1726. Its history really starts with the Duke of
Richmond and Gordon who developed it in 1827. This
is the only native Scottish gundog and is the largest of
the setters, very strong and an enthusiastic worker. It is
at its best
when hunting
game birds,
particularly
grouse, on the
moors. When
mature, it is a
very strong
dog with
exceptional
stamina.

German Shorthaired Pointer

Size: Height 60-65cm/24-26ins, weight 27-32kg/60-70lb. **Lifespan:** 12-14 years. **Identifying Features:** Short, thick coat, coarse to the touch. Colour is either solid liver, liver and white ticked or flecked, or the same variations in black and white. **Character:** Gentle, affectionate and even-tempered. **Pet Suitability:** Makes a good pet with little grooming requirement if exercised sufficiently and given adequate stimulation.

The German Shorthaired Pointer was developed from the German Pointer, a calm, slow-working dog with an excellent nose. English Pointer blood was introduced

in the 19th century to improve agility and scenting ability, and Spanish Pointer blood was also a possibility. It is now a firm favourite the world over, particularly with American field-trialists.

German Wirehaired Pointer

Size: Height 60-65cm/24-26ins, weight 27-32kg/60-70lb. **Lifespan:** 12-14 years. **Identifying Features:** Outer coat is thick and harsh with a dense undercoat. Colour is liver, liver and white or black and white. **Character:** Very loyal and obedient. **Pet Suitability:** Good-natured companion. Excellent family dog, very alert with a strong guarding instinct.

The German Wirehaired Pointer was deliberately created at the beginning of this century by German sportsmen. The breed is not very common outside its homeland where it is often used as a gamekeeper's dog, killing wild cats and foxes. Its ancestors may include the Pudelpointer, French Griffon and also the Airedale Terrier.

Irish Red and White Setters

> **Size:** Height 58-69cm/23-27ins, weight
> 27-32kg/60-70lb. **Lifespan:** 13 years. **Identifying
> Features:** Finely textured coat with good feathering.
> Pearly white colouring with solid red patches.
> **Character:** Intelligent, rather highly-strung,
> independent dogs. **Pet Suitability:** Reliable
> companion, though not easy to obedience train.

Irish shooting spaniels had evolved by the end of the 16th century. These were cross-bred with Bloodhounds to improve scenting ability, followed by inter-breeding with Black Pointers from Spain, which resulted in the longer-legged setter breed. A century ago, working Irish Setters were not always red, but mostly chestnut or red and white. Today the Red and Whites are being revived as a separate breed, more workmanlike and less glamorous than the Red Setter.

Irish Setter

Size: Height 64-69cm/25-27ins, weight 27-32kg/60-70lb. **Lifespan:** 13 years. **Identifying Features:** Coat is a glossy and rich chestnut colour, with abundant feathering on tops of ears, tail and legs. **Character:** Sweet, affectionate, but sometimes highly-strung. **Pet Suitability:** Very popular family dog. Playful and warm towards children. Needs adequate training and plenty of exercise. Not well-suited to urban life.

The Irish Setter is an immensely popular dog on both sides of the Atlantic, often nicknamed the Red Setter. Its ancestors are thought to include the Old Spanish Pointer, setting spaniels and early Scottish setters. Irish Setters like to gallop all day and do not take kindly to being kept on a leash in a town. They possess a good nose with a wide range, but it can be a little unpredictable. Very few are used today for work purposes; they are kept instead for their attractive appearance, and their warm affectionate nature.

Italian Spinone

Size: Height 61-66cm/24-26ins, weight 32-27kg/71-82lb. **Lifespan:** 12-13 years.
Identifying Features: Coat is tough, thick and slightly wiry. White colouring, with or without orange or brown markings. **Character:** Faithful and easygoing.
Pet Suitability: Excellent with children, fond of human companionship and family life. Loyal and courageous with good guarding instincts. Thrives on hard work and requires free-running exercise.

The Italian Spinone, or local varieties of this breed, has existed in the north of Italy for some centuries. Some believe it originated in France from the French

Pointer, the Porcelaine and the Barbet. The breed is said to be about 2000 years old and was originally used by marshland hunters because of its excellent swimming skills. The thick, wiry coat protects this rather large dog from freezing water. It is a good tracking dog and exhibits tremendous endurance.

Hungarian Vizsla

Size: Height 57-64cm/22.5-25ins, weight
22-30kg/48.5-66lb. **Lifespan:** 14-15 years.
Identifying Features: Lean head with square-ended
muzzle. Slightly oval eyes, darker in colour than coat.
Long, silky ears, rounded at tip, hanging close to
cheeks. Strong, muscular forelimbs, well-developed
thighs. Prominent breastbone. Rounded feet with
short toes and brown nails. Two types of coat,
shorthaired and wirehaired. Shorthaired is dense,
smooth and greasy to the touch. Wire-haired is
lustreless and harsh, forming a beard on muzzle.
Colour is russet gold. **Character:** Lively and
affectionate. **Pet Suitability:** Obedient, reliable and
easily trained with a strong protective instinct.

The Hungarian Vizsla was specially bred to hunt the
great plains of Hungary, pointing and retrieving
from land and water and hunting both fur and feather.
A dog of a similar type appears to have existed from the
18th century onwards and shows the influence of
cross-breeding with one of the Balkan pointers. The
wirehaired variety was developed only in the 1930s. It is
a very popular dog in Hungary and fairly well
established in Britain and America. It works in swamp
and marshland with enthusiasm and is normally trained
to search thoroughly within gunshot.

Large Munsterlander

> **Size:** Height 59-61cm/23-24ins, weight 25-29kg/55-65lb. **Lifespan:** 12-13 years. **Identifying Features:** Long, dense coat, neither curly nor coarse. Colouring is always black and white, ticked or flecked. **Character:** Affectionate and trustworthy. **Pet Suitability:** Thrives on close companionship but is not especially suited to urban life because of its drive and energy. Good with children and other pets. Easy to train.

The Large Munsterlander, a multi-purpose gundog with an excellent nose, was developed in Germany at the beginning of the century and is now becoming better known in England. The breed is both worked and shown in France and Germany. It is supposed to be an ideal dog for the rough shooting man and is very enthusiastic in the field. In Germany, this dog is used to hunt hare, fox and roe deer and works equally well on land or in water.

Pointer (English)

Size: Height 61-69cm/24-27ins, weight 20-30kg/44-66lb. **Lifespan:** 13-14 years. **Identifying Features:** Short, hard coat, usually lemon, orange, liver or black in colour, with or without white or tricolour markings. **Character:** Obedient and even-tempered. **Pet Suitability:** An ideal family companion, adaptable and alert. At its best in the open country, needs a good deal of activity.

At the beginning of the 18th century, the Spanish Pointer was imported into Britain for use in the

shooting field. A slow, methodical dog with an excellent nose, its pace suited those coping with muzzle–loading guns. As sporting guns improved however, a faster, more talented gundog was needed. By the time dog shows started in 1859, the Pointer was already a classic breed. Not so many pointers are now used in Britain for hunting, but in America it is a popular hunting dog and runs in many field trials.

Retriever (Chesapeake Bay)

> **Size:** Height 53-66cm/21-26ins, weight 25-34kg/55-75lb. **Lifespan:** 12-13 years.
> **Identifying Features:** Short, thick, tough coat which is oily and slightly wavy. Very distinctive colouring, shades of tan through to a dull tobacco. **Character:** Independent, affectionate and courageous. **Pet Suitability:** Makes a sound guardian and companion. Especially good with children. Loves water.

The Chesapeake Bay Retriever is a very tough American breed, displaying great courage and perseverance, said to have originated in 1807 when two puppies from Newfoundland were shipwrecked off the coast of Maryland. The dogs proved to be supreme hunters in freezing water and were mated with local gundogs to produce the Chesapeake strain, now used for retrieving ducks from the icy waters of Chesapeake Bay. Not many are seen in Britain.

Retriever (Curly-coated)

Size: Height 64-69cm/25-27ins, weight 32-36kg/70-80lb. **Lifespan:** 12-13 years. **Identifying Features:** Coat is a mass of crisp, small curls. Colour is black or liver. **Character:** Calm and even-tempered. **Pet Suitability:** Good family companion, intelligent with plenty of stamina. Reasonably easy to train. Good with children and other dogs.

The Curly-Coated Retriever is the largest and oldest of the retriever group. Related to the water spaniel and possibly the Newfoundland, it is excellent in water. The coat is slightly oily and traps air as an insulating layer when the dog is in water.

Although kept by gamekeepers in the 19th century, not many Curly-Coated Retrievers are seen today. It has a stronger guarding instinct than other retriever breeds and some have been successfully trained as guide dogs for the blind.

Retriever (Flat-coated)

Size: Height 56-61cm/22-24ins, weight 25-35kg/60-80lb. **Lifespan:** 12-14 years. **Identifying Features:** Dense coat, black or liver in colour. **Character:** Affectionate, warm disposition. **Pet Suitability:** Very active and versatile dogs, easy to train and handle.

Again, the Flat–Coated Retriever is not a well-known breed, although it was one of the most popular dogs kept by British gamekeepers at the turn of the century. By the 1920s, however, it had been totally eclipsed by the Labrador and Golden varieties. The Flat-coated Retriever was originally called a Wavy-coat and is believed to have come from Newfoundland stock, followed by Setter/Labrador cross-breeding. It is a superb flusher and an excellent retriever both on land and in water.

Retriever (Golden)

Size: Height 51-61cm/20-24ins, weight 27-36 kg/60-80lb. **Lifespan:** 13-15 years. **Identifying Features:** Coat is flat or wavy, dense and water-resistant, with feathering on legs and tail. Colour is any shade of gold or cream. **Character:** Responsible and friendly. **Pet Suitability:** Great family loyalty, and especially patient with children. Easy to train. Needs plenty of exercise, feeding and regular grooming.

Native to Britain, the Golden Retriever is popular both as a working and a show dog. It was bred to find, pick up and carry back hares or birds, without marking its quarry. The breed as we know it today was developed in the kennels of Lord Tweedmouth during the 1860s when he combined yellow flat-coated dogs with Tweed Water Spaniels and was first exhibited in 1908. The Golden Retriever is not an agressive dog in any way which makes it ideal for training as a guide to the blind.

Retriever (Labrador)

Size: Height 54-57cm/21.5-22.5ins, weight
25-34kg/55-75lb. **Lifespan:** 12-14 years.
Identifying Features: Short coat, hard to the touch,
usually in shades of yellow, black or chocolate.
Character: Good tempered and keen to please.
Pet Suitability: Very popular pet. Dependable,
adaptable and easy to train. Good with children and
other pets. Loves water. Needs lots of exercise.

Developed in the 19th century from Newfoundland
dogs, these retrievers first arrived in Britain on
fishing boats travelling to Poole harbour, Dorset. Locals
were impressed by the dog's ability to help fishermen
haul ashore the heavy nets and began keeping it as a
working animal. Sportsmen also began to appreciate it
as a valuable gundog suitable for wild-fowling. Now one
of the most popular breeds, the Labrador Retriever works
not only as a
gundog, but
also as an
impressive
'sniffer' dog
with police
forces world-
wide, and a
highly prized
guide dog.

Spaniel (American Cocker)

Size: Height 36-38cm/14-15in, weight 11-13kg/24-28lb. **Lifespan:** 13-14 years. **Identifying Features:** Slightly wavy coat of silky texture. Colour can be black or any solid colour, also particolour, with or without tan markings. **Character:** Warm and affectionate. **Pet Suitability:** Good family dog which enjoys lots of exercise. Very obedient and easy to train.

The American Cocker Spaniel was developed in America from the working English Cocker Spaniel. Prominent changes appeared in the 1920s when the dogs appeared with different heads and displayed more height at the shoulder and a longer neck. The American

Cocker is also distinguished by a long, silky, wavy coat which needs very careful grooming. Show dogs need professional clipping. They are now the most popular of all American-born breeds.

Spaniel (Clumber)

Size: Height 48-51cm/19-20ins, weight
29-36kg/65-80lb. **Lifespan:** 12-13 years.
Identifying Features: Abundant, close, silky, straight
coat. Colour is white, with lemon or orange markings.
Character: Highly intelligent and determined.
Pet Suitability: Good family dog, but not very popular.
Steady and reliable with a gentle nature. Easy to train.

The Clumber Spaniel is a very heavy, big-boned dog
whose ancestors may well include the Basset hound
and the St Bernard. Named after the Duke of Newcastle's
estate in Nottinghamshire, the Clumber is a slow

moving, leisurely
hunter once very
fashionable with
mature Edwardian
gentlemen. Today,
however, the fashion
is working spaniels
who can cover more
open territories at a
much faster pace
and the breed has
suffered a severe
decline in popularity
as a result. Most
are now only seen
at shows.

Spaniel (Cocker)

Size: Height 38-41cm/15-16ins, weight 13-15kg/28-32lb. **Lifespan:** 13-14 years. **Identifying Features:** Silky coat with plenty of feathering on legs and ears. Coat is a variety of colours. **Character:** Active, playful and affectionate. **Pet Suitability:** Good family pet. Easy to train. Lots of exercise required. Coat needs extensive grooming.

The Spaniel is believed to have originated in Spain some time before the 14th century. By the beginning of the 19th century, the small land spaniel breed was divided into two groups, 'starters', used to spring game, and 'cockers' used to hunt small game. Its success as a companion animal led to a decline in the emphasis on its working ability and it is now a very popular household companion throughout Eastern and Western Europe.

Spaniel (English Springer)

Size: Height 48-51cm/19-20ins, weight 22-24kg/49-53lb. **Lifespan:** 12-14 years. **Identifying Features:** Coat is close, straight and weather-resistant. Usually liver and white, black and white, or either of these colours with tan markings. **Character:** Friendly and happy. **Pet Suitability:** Easy to train, but not an ideal house pet. Requires regular grooming.

The English Springer Spaniel has a sound reputation as a working dog first and foremost, a good all-rounder in the shooting field, still used extensively for this purpose. Most are natural retrievers and hunters of unlimited stamina who like the water and who need a vast amount to do to keep them occupied. It loves human companionship but also has a great bond with dogs of its own kind. The English Spaniel is the tallest in the leg and is the raciest of all the British land spaniels.

Spaniel (Field)

Size: Height 51-58cm/20-23ins, weight 16-23kg/35-50lb. **Lifespan:** 12-13 years. **Identifying Features:** Long, flat, glossy coat, always solid-coloured, usually black or liver. **Character:** Unusually docile, yet independent. **Pet Suitability:** Not suited to urban life. Ideal as a shooting companion for the country dweller. Easy to train, good with children and other dogs.

Although quite popular in the early part of this century, the Field Spaniel is quite rare nowadays. After 1892, when it was recognized as a distinct breed, the Field Spaniel's shape was altered dramatically to produce a dog with a long back and short, heavy-boned legs. By the end of World War II, the dogs were almost extinct and by the time its shape had been corrected the Cocker had taken centre stage and the Field never recovered its popularity.

Spaniel (Irish Water)

Size: Height 51-58cm/20-23ins, weight 20-30kg/45-65lb. **Lifespan:** 12-14 years.
Identifying Features: Naturally oily coat is covered in crisp ringlets, forming a pronounced top-knot on skull. Colour is always dark liver with a purplish hue.
Character: Initially aloof, but affectionate and humorous. **Pet Suitability:** Not ideal as a domestic pet; loves water and open countryside. Easy to train and highly intelligent, but needs a competent handler to get the best out of it.

Although the first precise description and illustration of the Irish Water Spaniel appears as late as 1790, the breed is thought to have a long history as a gundog going back over a 1000 years. The animal's evolution

may have involved inter-breeding between Poodles, Irish Setters and possibly Curly-coated Retrievers. This spaniel has an excellent nose, makes an excellent wildfowler and versatile gundog for all types of shooting.

Spaniel (Sussex)

Size: Height 38–41cm/15–16ins, weight
18–23kg/40–50lb. **Lifespan:** 12–13 years.
Identifying Features: Abundant and flat coat with a
weather-resistant undercoat. Colour is rich golden
liver. **Character:** Friendly disposition.
Pet Suitability: Not ideal as a household pet. Strong
working ability. Easy to train. Good with children and
other dogs. Regular grooming required.

It is a strongly–built dog, very rare in its native Britain.
In 1946 only two Sussex Spaniels were registered with
the British Kennel Club, and fewer still exist in
America. Originally, it was bred and used locally in the
English county of Sussex to hunt slowly through the
thickest cover. Where other spaniels are silent, the
Sussex was expected to give tongue when on the scent.
Experienced owners could tell whether their dog was
after fur or feather by variations in the dog's tone.

Spaniel (Welsh Springer)

Size: Height 46-48cm/18-19ins, weight 16-20kg/35-45lb. **Lifespan:** 12-14 years. **Identifying Features:** Flat, silky coat, never wiry or wavy. Feathering on forelegs, hindlegs, ears and tail. Colour is always rich red and white. **Character:** Warm and affectionate. **Pet Suitability:** Needs an owner with lots of energy and enthusiasm for exercising. Easy to train. Good with children and other animals. Regular grooming required.

First recognized as a distinct breed in 1902, the Welsh Springer Spaniel is somewhat smaller than its English cousins and is thought to share the same ancestry as the Brittany. A very enthusiastic retriever from water and a good game-finder with plenty of stamina, the Welsh Springer Spaniel has always been regarded as a superb working dog.

Weimaraner

Size: Height 56-69cm/22-27 ins, weight 32-39kg/70.5-86lb. **Lifespan:** 12-13 years. **Identifying Features:** Silver grey, sleek coat with metallic sheen. **Character:** Alert and obedient with a strong hunting instinct. **Pet Suitability:** Demands an active owner to provide exercise. Not particularly suited to children.

A grey dog of similar appearance to the Weimaraner was painted by Van Eyck in the early 15th century, providing one of the earliest records of the breed. It is thought that the dogs were developed by crossing Bloodhounds with local pointers and hunting dogs. The distinctive colour of the coat has earned it the nickname of 'grey ghost'.

THE
❧ TERRIER GROUP ❧

Group Features

Most of the world's terriers evolved in Britain from various hound breeds. The object of breeders was to produce a dog that would fearlessly go to ground after burrowing animals such as badgers, rats, rabbits or foxes on their home territory. During the 18th and 19th centuries the popularity of these tough, working dogs increased in industrial areas and many were kept to control vermin in rural towns and for working down the mines.

By the 1800s different regional variations of short-legged terriers were being bred throughout the country, including the Border, Yorkshire, Skye and Cairn terriers. Man further refined some breeds and enhanced the aggressive instinct to produce dogs such as the English and Staffordshire bull terriers that would bait large animals or fight other dogs.

• Roman invaders of Britain in the first century AD christened these dogs 'terrarii'. 'Terra' means 'the earth' in Latin, a description which befits the dogs' powerful urge to tunnel into the ground.

• Twenty–nine breeds of terrier exist in Britain today.

• The terrier spirit is fiery, tenacious and independent. They come in a great variety of shapes, sizes and coat colours.

Rather like a hound, a terrier should have a good voice so that it can keep in contact with the huntsmen when it is in the field. Once the dog has marked its quarry and has gone underground, it should keep on barking to let the men on the surface know its whereabouts. They can then dig down and haul out the fox or badger.

Airedale Terrier

Size: Height 56-61cm/22-24in, weight 20-23kg/44-50lb. **Lifespan:** 13 years.
Identifying Features: Hard, dense and wiry coat. Colour is black or dark grizzle, with tan head and legs.
Character: Outgoing, confident, but never aggressive.
Pet Suitability: Requires firm handling and plenty of physical exercise. Excellent guard dog. Not good with other dogs. Hunting urge may be difficult to suppress.

The Airedale, the largest of the terriers, comes from Yorkshire and is generally considered a mixture of Otterhound, Welsh Harrier and various local terriers. Known originally as the 'Waterside' or 'Warfedale Terrier', it excelled at water work and as an all-round sports dog, being used to catch rabbits, kill rats, mark and retrieve game, work on the farm, and serve as a family guard. Nowadays, the Airedale has suffered a substantial decline in popularity but it is still fairly widely used in Germany as a police dog.

Australian Terrier

Size: Height 25.5cm/10ins, weight 5-6kg/12-14lb.
Lifespan: 14 years. **Identifying Features:** Harsh, straight, dense topcoat. Short, soft-textured undercoat. Colour is steel blue or dark grey blue with rich tan markings on leg or body. Can also be sandy or red. **Character:** Obedient and extrovert. **Pet Suitability:** Good companion and reasonably easy to train. Will not easily tolerate cats or other dogs.

This terrier was first shown in Australia in 1899 and its ancestors are undoubtedly a mixture of small terriers, including Cairns, Dandies and Irish, with a distinct Yorkshsire Terrier influence. The end result of this inter-breeding is a very small, agile working dog with a rugged, hard-bitten appearance, keen eyesight and quick reflexes. It is happy to take on rats, small game, snakes, or any other vermin.

Bedlington Terrier

Size: Height 38-43cm/15-17ins, weight
8-10kg/17-23lb. **Lifespan:** 14-15 years. **Identifying
Features:** Narrow skull with long, tapering jaw. White,
silky top-knot. Small, deep-set eyes. Low-set ears with
fringe of whitish silky hair at tip. Long neck with deep
base. Straight forelegs, muscular hindquarters. Deep
chest. Long, hare feet. Low-set tail, thick at root.
Thick coat with a tendency to twist. Colour is liver,
sandy or blue, with or without tan. **Character:** Spirited,
with a strong sporting instinct. **Pet Suitability:** Needs
regular mental and physical stimulation. Full of
courage when roused and a good watchdog.

The Bedlington Terrier has existed for some 200
years and has a lamb like appearance very different
from most other terriers. It
may be an ancestor of the
Dandie Dinmont, but is
believed to have been
interbred with the Whippet
to improve sporting ability.
It is a tall and graceful
terrier with long legs, long
neck and arched loins. It
first appeared in the show
ring in 1869 but has
suffered a decline in
popularity this century.

Border Terrier

Size: Height 25-28cm/10-11ins, weight
5-7kg/11.5-15lb. **Lifespan:** 13-14 years.
Identifying Features: Harsh, dense coat with thick
undercoat. Colour is red, wheaten, grizzle and tan, or
blue and tan. **Character:** Active and sporting.
Pet Suitability: Excellent family dog with
extremely affable nature. Friendly with other dogs.
Requires regular exercise but only a moderate
amount of grooming.

The Border Terrier is a close relative of both the
Dandie Dinmont and the Bedlington and originated
in the Border country between England and Scotland
where it was used in the hunt to go to ground after
foxes. It needed to be small for this purpose, yet strong
enough to tackle its prey and keep up with the
horses. This
dog makes
an excellent
small sporting
companion,
keen to
challenge
anything that
moves.

Bull Terrier

Size: Height 53-56cm/21-22ins, weight 24-28kg/52-62lb. **Lifespan:** 11-13 years.
Identifying Features: Short, harsh, glossy coat. Colour is pure white, black, brindle, red, fawn, or tricolour.
Character: Even-tempered and courageous.
Pet Suitability: Good family dog and successful with children if carefully trained. Should never be encouraged to fight. Needs plenty of stimulation. Not ideal with other pets. Good watchdog.

The Bull Terrier owes its origin to a Mr James Hinks of Birmingham who crossed the White English Terrier with bulldogs, at a time when dog-fighting flourished in England. The bulldog itself proved too cumbersome in the dog pit and the need arose for a strain with greater speed and agility which still retained the courage and tenacity of a fighting dog. Still recognized as the gladiator of the canine race, the Bull Terrier is a strongly-built dog which appears today in many varieties, all stemming from a common ancestry.

Cairn Terrier

Size: Height 25-31cm/10-12ins, weight
6-7.5kg/13-16lb. **Lifespan:** 14 years.
Identifying Features: Double coat with profuse, harsh
outer coat and short, close undercoat. Colour is
cream, wheaten, red, grey, or nearly black. **Character:**
Fearless and gay disposition. **Pet Suitability:** One of
the easiest terriers to obedience train. Affectionate
towards children and an excellent guard.

The Cairn Terrier is a small, short-legged sporting
dog from Scotland; a hardy, intelligent breed still
used to work with hounds. Cairn Terriers were originally
used to keep down the numbers of vermin and to
hunt fox, otter or badgers. To do this they
had to be small enough to go underground
and agile enough to wriggle their way
through rocks and crannies. The Cairn
Terrier's coat is tough and waterproof to
withstand harsh
Scottish weather
conditions.

Dandie Dinmont

Size: Height 20-28cm/8-11ins, weight
8-11kg/18-24lb. **Lifespan:** 13-14 years. **Identifying
Features:** Double coat with harsher topcoat. Colour is
mustard or pepper. **Character:** Loyal and friendly.
Pet Suitability: Even-tempered house dog, good with
both children and adults. Formidable watchdog.

The Dandie Dinmont is another terrier from
Scotland with a weasel-like shape, its long, flexible
body almost twice the length of its height. The breed
was renowned for its persistence and fearlessness when
hunting otter, fox and badger. Today's dog is still as
courageous as ever. The deep resonant bark gives the
impression of a larger breed.

Fox Terrier (Smooth and Wire)

Smooth

> **Size:** Height 38.5-39.5cm/15ins,
> weight 7-8kg/16-18lb. **Lifespan:** 13-14 years.
> **Identifying Features:** Flat, moderately narrow skull.
> Round, dark, deep-set eyes. Straight, flat, abundant
> coat. Colour is white, white and tan, or black and tan.
> **Character:** Friendly and fearless. **Pet Suitability:** More
> suited to rural life than urban. Fiery-spirited, difficult
> to train. Enjoys challenging other dogs, although quite
> good with children. Plenty of exercise required.

Smooth and Wire Fox Terriers are now considered two separate breeds although they share the same original function, to travel with the foxhound pack and to bolt the fox from its hiding place to the waiting hounds. The origins of the dogs are obscure since the term Fox Terrier was used to describe a wide range of terriers. Wire and Smooth varieties were first properly recorded in the 1870s.

Wire

> **Size:** Height 38.5-39.5cm/15ins,
> weight 7-8kg/16-18lb. **Lifespan:** 13-14 years.
> **Identifying Features:** Dense, very wiry coat with a
> soft, woolly undercoat. Colour is white, white and
> tan, or white and black. **Character:** Alert and
> courageous. **Pet Suitability:** More suited to rural life
> than urban. A fiery-spirited terrier difficult to train.
> Enjoys challenging other dogs; can be quite snappy.

These terriers were required to display strength and
endurance in order to face an opponent in the
narrow confines of an underground
lair. They have now left their
working past behind them.
The Smooth Fox Terrier
was a popular dog in
the early part of this
century but the
Wire became the
more fashionable
breed in the
1930s.

Glen of Imaal Terrier

Size: Height 35.3-36.5cm/14ins, weight
15.5-16.5kg/34-36lb. **Lifespan:** 13-14 years.
Identifying Features: Harsh-textured topcoat with soft
undercoat. Colour is blue, brindle or wheaten.
Character: Gentle, docile, yet very courageous when
roused. **Pet Suitability:** Equally content to live in
town or country. Not good with other dogs.
Impressive guards. Minimum exercise required.

Named after a valley in County Wicklow, Ireland,
the Glen of Imaal Terrier was once a fierce fox and
badger hunter and was also bred for dog fighting. This
sturdy and adaptable terrier first appeared in the showrings
in 1933. Nowadays it has a more relaxed temperament
and is kept as a companion rather than a working dog,
although it still relishes a good fight if provoked.

Irish Terrier

Size: Height 46-48cm/18-19ins, weight
11-12kg/25-27lb. **Lifespan:** 13 years.
Identifying Features: Hard, wiry topcoat wtih fine,
soft undercoat. Colour is usually red, wheaten-red, or
yellow-red. **Character:** Good-tempered with humans,
but exceptionally hostile to other dogs.
Pet Suitability: Good watchdog and overall
companion but needs very firm handling. Suited to
either town or country.

An excellent water dog, hunter and ratter, the
Irish Terrier is nicknamed 'Daredevil' because of its
fiery temperament which is combined with a merry,
affectionate streak. Primarily a companion dog
nowadays, it is still more racy than most terriers and will
not readily back down from a fight. Like most terriers,

this dog
will soon
get into
mischief if
left idle.

Kerry Blue Terrier

Size: Height 46-48cm/18-19ins, weight
15-17kg/33-37lb. **Lifespan:** 14 years. **Identifying
Features:** Soft, silky and abundant coat. Colour is any
shade of blue. **Character:** Disciplined and spirited.
Pet Suitability: A good all-round terrier and a suitable
household pet, but extremely argumentative with
other canines. Good guarding instincts.

First shown in 1915 in Killarney, Ireland, the Kerry
Blue Terrier was originally used for herding cattle,
catching rats, guarding the farm and for going to
ground after fox and badger. Its ancestors may well
include the Bedlington, Dandie Dinmont and the Irish
Terrier. It likes water and some of these terriers have
been trained to retrieve. The pups are born with a black
coat which lightens to a blue shade after about a year.

Lakeland Terrier

Size: Height 33-38cm/13-15ins, weight 7-8kg/15-17lb. **Lifespan:** 13-14 years. **Identifying Features:** Dense, harsh, weather-resistant coat. Colour is wheaten, red, blue, black, black and tan, or blue and tan. **Character:** Bold, friendly and self-confident. **Pet Suitability:** A stubborn, wilful terrier that needs a patient owner. Not tolerant of other dogs and best suited to rural life. Good watchdog.

The Lakeland Terrier is a dark-coloured hunting terrier, bred in the Lake District where it was given many different names according to the region in which it was found, including the Cumberland, the Patterdale and the Fell Terrier. In 1923 the various dogs were standardized and refined to produce the Lakeland Terrier, a dog shorter in the leg and somewhat heavier than its predecessors.

Manchester Terrier

Size: Height 38-41cm/15-16ins, weight
5-10kg/11-22lb. **Lifespan:** 13-14 years.
Identifying Features: Short, glossy coat, firm in
texture. Colour is jet black and rich mahogany.
Character: Discerning, occasionally short-tempered,
yet loyal. **Pet Suitability:** Easy to care for, compact
dog. Lively and robust. Good watchdog.

Once simply called the Black and Tan, the Manchester Terrier is one of the few smooth-coated terrier breeds. A wire-haired version existed, but has become extinct, leaving behind traces of its ancestry in breeds like the Airedale. The Manchester Terrier was only given its name in the 1920s, though it is one of the oldest terrier types. It has never been a very popular breed and its numbers declined substantially when rat baiting became unfashionable.

Scottish Terrier

Size: Height 25-28cm/10-11ins, weight 8.5-10.5kg/19-23lb. **Lifespan:** 13-14 years. **Identifying Features:** Coat is double with a dense, wiry topcoat and a soft, dense undercoat. Colour is black, brindle or wheaten. **Character:** Courageous, loyal and faithful. **Pet Suitability:** An excellent guardian. Terrier temperament may make training difficult.

The Scottish Terrier, previously known as the Aberdeen, is the powerful heavyweight among the short-legged terriers, once used to hunt for badger, fox and vermin. Fiercely loyal to home and master, the Scottish Terrier is essentially a companion dog nowadays,

although it has a reputation for being very stubborn and independent which can be frustrating for some owners.

Norfolk and Norwich Terriers

Size: Height 25-26cm/10ins, weight 5-5.5kg/11-12lb.
Lifespan: 14 years. **Identifying Features:** Broad skull
with wedge-shaped muzzle. Dark, oval-shaped eyes.
V-shaped ears, dropping forward in Norfolk, erect in
Norwich. Short, powerful and straight forelegs.
Strong, well-muscled hindquarters. Coat is hard, wiry
and straight. Longer and rougher on neck and
shoulders. Colour is all shades of red, wheaten, black
and tan, or grizzle. **Character:** Alert and fearless,
loveable and not quarrelsome. **Pet Suitability:** Happy
in either town or country and good with children.
Minimum grooming required, moderate exercise.
Norwich is more difficult to train than the Norfolk.
Both make formidable watchdogs.

Norfolk and Norwich Terriers are amongst the
smallest of the terrier group and share the same
ancestry, probably a mixture of Irish, Border and Cairn
Terriers. They are Britain's only short-legged terrier and
are identical in appearance, apart from the carriage of
the ears. Both types, drop- and prick-eared, were
originally used to kill vermin and were classed as
Norwich terriers until 1965 when the British Kennel
Club decided to call the drop-eared type the Norfolk
Terrier. In America, both types are still known as
Norwich Terriers.

Sealyham Terrier

Size: Height 25-31cm/(10-12ins, weight 8-9kg/18-20lb. **Lifespan:** 14 years. **Identifying Features:** Coat is wiry, long and weather-resistant. Colour is pure white, occasionally with markings in either lemon, brown or badger on head and ears.
Character: Independent and workmanlike.
Pet Suitability: Needs experienced handler who will treat it firmly. Strong hunting urge. Not ideal with other dogs or children.

A comparatively new breed, the Sealyham Terrier is a native of Wales, created by Captain John Edwards of Sealyham House in Pembrokeshire in the mid-19th century. This dog was specifically bred for badger and otter hunting and has strong jaws and a hard white coat, essential for working in thickets or in water. The Sealyham is a friendly terrier, but it also comes with a stubborn streak.

Skye Terrier

Size: Height 25-26cm/10ins, weight 8.5-10.5kg/19-23lb. **Lifespan:** 13 years. **Identifying Features:** Long, straight topcoat, short and woolly undercoat. Colour is black, cream, fawn or grey, always with black ears and nose. **Character:** Dignified, sensitive and rather aloof. **Pet Suitability:** Time-consuming and impractical household pet. Not ideal with children.

The Skye Terrier was not given its name until 1861 although it has been popular in its Hebridean birthplace for centuries and was at one time a firm favourite with the royal courts of Scotland and England. Originally used for badger, otter and weasel tracking, it is a very dramatic looking dog. The long flowing coat is low to the ground and demands a great deal of patience and experience to maintain which is possibly the reason why this breed has not retained the popularity it once enjoyed, except in show circles.

Soft-Coated Wheaten Terrier

Size: Height 46-48cm/18-19ins, weight 16-20kg/35-45lb. **Lifespan:** 13-14 years. **Identifying Features:** Coat is soft, silky and loosely waved or curled. Colour is wheaten. **Character:** Confident, good-humoured and even-tempered. **Pet Suitability:** Suited to both urban and rural life. Quite easy to train, loyal and good with children.

The Soft-Coated Wheaten Terrier has a long history as a working dog in the Munster area of south-west Ireland and can be traced back 200 years or more. The Kerry Blue is said to have descended from the Wheaten and both breeds were originally used for hunting, herding and guarding. The dogs are slightly smaller and stockier than the Kerry variety, and were not officially recognized in Britain until 1939.

Staffordshire Bull Terrier

Size: Height 36-41cm/14-16ins, weight 11-17kg/24-38lb. **Lifespan:** 11-12 years. **Identifying Features:** Smooth, close-cut coat. Colours can be red, fawn, white, black or blue, or any combination of these with added white. Any shade of brindle or brindle with white. **Character:** Highly intelligent and fearless. **Pet Suitability:** Particularly affectionate with children and a devoted, loyal family pet. Requires a responsible owner, committed to careful training.

Not unlike the Bull Terrier, the Staffordshire Bull Terrier is descended from large bull-mastiff dogs. During the early 19th century, when dog fighting became popular as a sport, terrier blood was added to the mastiff breeds to produce more aggressive canines. The Staffordshire Bull Terrier was not properly recognized until 1935 because of the wide variety in type and appearance and its aggressive reputation.

Welsh Terrier

Size: Height 36-39cm/14-15.5 ins, weight
9-10kg/20-22lb. **Lifespan:** 14 years. **Identifying
Features:** Coat is wiry, very close and abundant.
Colour is black and tan or black grizzle and tan.
Character: Happy, game and fearless. **Pet Suitability:**
Reasonably easy to obedience train. Fairly good with
other dogs and a formidable watchdog. Plenty of
physical exercise is essential.

The Welsh Terrier is one of the oldest varieties of
terriers, originating in North Wales in the 1760s.
Often confused with the Lakeland Terrier, it was
originally used by Welsh farmers to hunt for hill foxes
with various other hounds. For this reason it often
prefers to
hunt in
packs (a rare
occurrence
for most
terriers), and
is not very
quarrelsome,
having
learned to
tolerate
other dogs.

West Highland White Terrier

> **Size:** Height 25-28cm/10-11ins, weight
> 7-10kg/15-22lb. **Lifespan:** 14 years. **Identifying
> Features:** Harsh topcoat, with a softer, furry
> undercoat. Colour is always white, except for black
> nose, eyes, paws and toe-nails. **Character:** Self-reliant
> and wilful. **Pet Suitability:** Not an easy first dog.
> Good watchdog.

Known affectionately as 'The Westie', the West
Highland White Terrier seems to have been bred
from a variety of other small working terriers popular in
Scotland at the beginning of this century. It has also

been suggested that
it was a cast-off from
Cairn litters,
selectively bred by
the Malcolm family
of Scotland. This
dog excelled in otter
and fox hunting in
the past and
although it is no
longer widely used in
this capacity, it still
likes to chase the
odd rabbit.

THE
~ UTILITY GROUP ~

Group Features

The use of dogs as guards, herders, gundogs, hunters or toy companions is the broad basis of classification today. The Utility Group is a miscellaneous collection of

breeds, however, which cannot be slotted neatly into any of the other five categories. Many choose to call these dogs 'special dogs'; they are certainly some of the more unusual and interesting breeds, and in America they are known as 'Non-sporting dogs'.

Many of these dogs are very ancient breeds, created for some particular purpose in the past which they have since left behind. The Poodle, for example, which descended originally from a German gundog, was once a water-retriever and also a herd-guarder, but nowadays it is almost exclusively a companion animal.

Some of the Utility Group such as the Alaska Sled Dog below are still used primarily as working dogs. The Bulldog dates back to the 16th century and was specifically developed for bull-baiting. When the sport was outlawed in 1835 the Bulldog lost its original function and modern breeds are somewhat gentler than their forerunners.

Boston Terrier

Size: Height 38-43cm/15-17ins, weight 4.5-11.5kg/10-25lb. **Lifespan:** 13 years. **Identifying Features:** Colour is usually brindle and white, or black and white, with markings in a definite pattern. **Character:** Strong-willed, yet considerate. **Pet Suitability:** Good with children. Enjoys the company of humans. Happy to live in either town or country.

The Boston Terrier does not really belong to the Terrier Group and is placed in the Utility Group in Britain and in the Non-sporting Group in America. It was bred originally as a fighting dog in the region around Boston, but the modern variety is far less aggressive than its ancestors. It is a mixture of many breeds, including one of the smooth-coated terriers, but the Bulldog influence is prominent. Three sizes exist in its native America – under 6.8kg /15lb, 6.8-9kg/15-20lb and over 9kg/20lb.

Bulldog

Size: Height 31-36cm/12-14ins, weight
23-25kg/50-55lb. **Lifespan:** 9-11 years.
Identifying Features: Short, close coat usually in
whole or smut colours. Black or black and tan
undesirable. **Character:** Fierce in appearance, but
warm and affectionate. **Pet Suitability:** Good with
children, yet can be obstinate.

Ancestors of the modern Bulldog were bred for
bull-baiting and looked more like the present-day
Staffordshire Bull Terrier. The deep underjaw enabled
the Bulldog to hang
on to its prey with a
vice-like grip and still
manage to breathe.
The Bulldog is still
considered a symbol
of courage and
strength nowadays,
although the breed
suffers a short life-
span. Its exaggerated
shape and the
excessive wrinkles on
the face are as
popular as ever with
dog owners.

Chow Chow

Size: Height 46-56cm/18-22ins, weight 19-32kg/40-70lb. **Lifespan:** 11-12 years.
Identifying Features: Coat either rough or smooth. Rough coats are profuse and stand-off. Smooth coats are short and up-standing. Colour is usually solid and includes black, red, blue, fawn, cream or white.
Character: Loyal, yet aloof. **Pet Suitability:** An excellent guard, but strong–minded. Not good with children.

Once reared for human consumption throughout Mongolia and Manchuria, the Chow Chow is the Chinese version of the Spitz type of dog with a lion-like appearance. The first chows to reach the Western world arrived back with the explorers of the Dutch East Indies in the 18th century, although the breed did not become

firmly established in the West until early this century. The bluish-black tongue and lining of the mouth is a unique feature.

Dalmation

> **Size:** Height 50-61cm/20-24ins, weight 23-25kg/50-55lb. **Lifespan:** 12-14 years. **Identifying Features:** Coat is short and hard, yet glossy. Base colour is always pure white with dense black or liver brown spots evenly-spaced and slightly smaller on the extremities. **Character:** Intelligent and deeply affectionate. **Pet Suitability:** Good family pet for the energetic type. Can be deaf due to a genetic problem.

The Dalmation is reputed to have been brought by Gypsies from northern India to Dalmatia where it was used to give advance warning of invading Turks. By the 17th century, it appeared in hunting pictures throughout Europe and was depicted as a household companion in Dutch paintings. Dalmation pups are normally born white and the spots develop after about a fortnight.

French Bulldog

Size: Height 30.5-31.5cm/12ins, weight 10-13kg/22-28lb. **Lifespan:** 11-12 years. **Identifying Features:** Over-sized, square head with flat muzzle and undershot mouth. Oval-shaped, obliquely set eyes. Small, erect, triangular-shaped ears. Strong and muscular hindlegs, slightly shorter than forelegs. Small, compact feet. Very short tail. Close coat, smooth and fine in texture. Colours include brindle, pied and fawn. **Character:** Playful and friendly. **Pet Suitability:** Comfort-loving dogs, suitable for urban life. Good family pets, affectionate towards children. Minimum grooming required.

Also known as the Frenchie, the French Bulldog has been in existence for just over a century. It originated in France, but is also now quite popular in other parts of Europe and also America. Most attempts to produce a miniature bulldog were unsuccessful and the French Bulldog is the only one to have established itself.

Japanese Akita

Size: Height 60-71cm/24-28ins, weight
34-50kg/75-110lb. **Lifespan:** 10-12 years.
Identifying Features: Topcoat is coarse, thick and
stand-off. Undercoat is fine and dense. Can be any
colour, including white, brindle or pinto.
Character: Loyal and courageous. **Pet Suitability:**
Needs an experienced owner. Not easily trained.
Unsuitable for households with children.

The Japanese Akita is the largest Japanese spitz breed,
known to be in existence for at least 300 years. The
Akita is a very dominant and imposing dog. Ownership
in the past was restricted to royalty who used the dog to
hunt wild boar,
deer and the
Japanese Black
Bear. It was also
once used for
pit-fighting.
Modern dogs
are used for
police and army
work and they
also make
excellent guards.

Japanese Spitz

Size: Height 30-36cm/12-14ins, weight 5-6kg/11-13lb. **Lifespan:** 12 years. **Identifying Features:** Topcoat straight and stand-off, undercoat dense and short. Colour is always pure white. **Character:** Bold and energetic. **Pet Suitability:** Good family pet. Easy to train, but not ideal for young children. Has a reputation for being rather outspoken. Daily grooming is required and moderate exercise.

The Japanese Spitz bears a striking resemblance to the Pomeranian, and also to the Samoyed. It is slowly becoming better known outside of Japan where it is thought to have been bred from other spitz breeds, possibly the Finnish spitz and Norwegian Buhund.

Keeshond

Size: Height 43-48cm/17-19ins, weight 25-30kg/55-66lb. **Lifespan:** 12-14 years. **Identifying Features:** Harsh, off-standing outer coat. Soft, thick undercoat. Colour is a mixture of grey and black. **Character:** Courageous with marked guarding instinct. **Pet Suitability:** Suited to both town and countryside. Need experienced handlers. Requires a good deal of exercise and grooming.

The Keeshond, a spitz breed from Holland, is named after the leader of the Dutch rebels who challenged the ruling House of Orange. By the 19th century, most farms and barges had such dogs. They first reached the show ring in various countries in 1925.

Lhaso Apso

Size: Height 25-28cm/10-11ins, weight
6-7kg/13-15lb. **Lifespan:** 13-14 years.
Identifying Features: Good whiskers and beard, hair
traditionally falling over the eyes. Gold and honey are
the preferred colours, but dark grizzle, smoke, black,
particolour, white or brown are not unusual.
Character: Highly intelligent, yet somewhat aloof.
Pet Suitability: Good family dog. Excellent guard. Coat
needs a lot of grooming. Minimum exercise required.

The Lhaso Apso is one of four
Tibetan breeds, originally
associated with the ancient
monasteries of Tibet and
probably descended from
the long-coated herding
dogs of Asia. These dogs
were believed to bring
good luck and were also
believed to have religious
significance. They have
always been treated with
the greatest respect in their
homeland where it is
considered a great honour
to be presented with
one as a gift.

Poodle

Size: (Standard) Height 37.5-38.5cm/15ins, weight 20.5-32kg/45-70lb. **Lifespan:** 11-15 years.
Identifying Features: Profuse, dense coat of harsh texture which does not moult but needs regular brushing. Traditional 'lion clip' should be adhered to. Colours are solid, including white, cream, brown, black, apricot, blue and silver. **Character:** Dependable, even-tempered and high-spirited.
Pet Suitability: Easy to train, good family dog. Reliable guard, affectionate towards children.

The Poodle was originally used in Europe as a gundog to retrieve game from water. The modern Poodle is one of the most popular companion breeds. It is a happy, intelligent, high-spirited dog, keen to play and to entertain. Three Poodle types now exist, differing only in size. The Standard Poodle is the largest of the group.

Miniature Poodle ▲ *Toy Poodle* ▼

Miniature and Toy Poodles

Size: (Miniature) Height 28-38cm/11-15ins, weight 12-14kg/26-30lb. (Toy) Height 25-28cm/10-11ins, weight 6.5-7.5kg/14-16.5lb. **Lifespan:** 14-17 years.
Character: Responsive, thoughtful and lively.
Pet Suitability: Good companion and adaptable to most human lifestyles. Has a reputation for being exhibitionist.

The Miniature Poodle is more popular than the Standard Poodle probably because far less time is needed for grooming. Standard Poodles were probably taken from Germany to France at least 500 years ago. Both Miniature and Toy Poodles became exceptionally popular in the 1950s and 1960s. The Toy Poodle is now the most popular of all the group.

Schipperke

Size: Height 22-33cm/9-13ins, weight 3-8kg/7-18lb.
Lifespan: 12-13 years. **Identifying Features:** Broad,
flat skull. Dark brown eyes, small black nose.
Moderately long, erect ears. Strong, full, rather short
neck. Broad, deep chest. Small, cat-like feet. Tail
customarily docked. Abundant, dense coat. Smooth
on head, ears and legs. Thick around neck, forming a
mane, harsh elsewhere. Colour is usually black.
Character: Intelligent, loyal and energetic.
Pet Suitability: A conveniently-sized, reliable
household companion, although not really suited to
an idle life. Formidable guard. Easily trained, but not
ideally behaved with other dogs.

Another of the spitz breeds, the
Schipperke was created in
Belgium about 150 years ago.
It is an extremely
vigilant and eager
breed, originally
used on canal boats
as a guard dog and
rat-catcher. Its name
translates as 'little skipper'.
The head is rather fox-like
and it has a shrill, piercing
bark which gives obvious
warning of strangers.

Schnauzer

> **Size:** (Giant) Height 59-70cm/23.5-27.5ins,
> weight 32-35kg/70-77lb. (Standard) Height
> 45-50cm/18-20ins, weight 14.5-15.5kg/32-34lb.
> **Lifespan:** (Giant) 11-12 years, (Standard) 12-14 years.
> **Identifying Features:** Coat is short and wiry. Dense
> undercoat essential. Colours are pure black or pepper
> and salt shades. **Character:** Alert and reliable. **Pet
> Suitability:** Good companion dog. Reasonably easy to
> train and happy to live in either town or country. May
> be troublesome with other dogs. Demands regular
> physical exercise.

Three types of Schnauzers exist today, the Giant or Riesenschnauzer (below right), the Standard Schnauzer (above right) and the Miniature Schnauzer. The first of the group, the Giant or Riesenschnauzer, is an old breed from Bavaria, developed by increasing the size of the standard Schnauzer. Today the Giant breed's popularity has declined substantially but it is still used by some as a guard dog and is recognized in Germany as a valuable police and service dog.

The Standard Schnauzer from which the miniature and giant breeds later evolved is a sturdily built dog, of great stamina and endurance. It was the first of the group to make an impression outside its German homeland. Its fearlessness made it an ideal message carrier during war-time and it is still an excellent livestock dog and a vigilant guard.

Miniature Schnauzer

Size: Height 30-36cm/12-14ins, weight
6-7kg/13-15lb. **Lifespan:** 14 years.
Identifying Features: Harsh, wiry coat with dense
undercoat. All pepper and salt colours in even
porportions, or pure black, or black and silver.
Character: Well-balanced, calm and adaptable.
Pet Suitability: Easily trained and good with children
and other dogs. An excellent guard, but sometimes
prone to nervousness. Coat needs regular stripping.

Also known as the Zwergschnauzer, the Miniature
Schnauzer descends from the Giant and Standard
varieties with added Affenpinscher and Miniature
Pinscher blood. In America and Canada the Miniature
Schnauzer is classed as a terrier.

Shih-Tzu

Size: Height 25-27cm/10-11ins, weight 5-7kg/10-16lb. **Lifespan:** 13-14 years.
Identifying Features: Coat may be any colour. White blaze on forehead and white tip to tail highly desirable. **Character:** Alert and active.
Pet Suitability: Adaptable family pet. Minimum exercise required, but regular grooming essential.

The Shih-Tzu is one of a number of 'lion-dog' breeds originating in the Far East. The lion features prominently in Buddhist mythology and was believed to be the animal Buddha himself kept as a pet. The modern Shih-Tzu is almost certainly the result of cross-breeding between ancient Tibetan dogs and Chinese Pekes.

Tibetan Spaniel

Size: Height 24.5-25.5cm/10ins, weight 4-7kg/9-15lb.
Lifespan: 13-14 years. **Identifying Features:** Silky topcoat, longer over the shoulders. Fine, dense undercoat. Can be any solid colour or mixture of colours. **Character:** Loyal, yet independent.
Pet Suitability: Highly intelligent, but not very easy to train. Safe with children and a good family guard. Needs a regular amount of exercise.

For well over 1000 years, Far Eastern countries have produced a number of small, snub-nosed dogs, many of which are depicted on pottery and in silk paintings. Ancient Buddhist cultures held these animals in very high regard. They were reputedly used to turn the Buddhist prayer wheels and were valued also for their intelligence and companionship. The Tibetan Spaniel qualifies for a place among Toy Dog breeds because of its size, but the British Kennel Club does not class it as such.

Tibetan Terrier

Size: Height 36-41cm/14-16ins, weight 8-14kg/18-30lb. **Lifespan:** 13-14 years. **Identifying Features:** Profuse top-coat, either straight or wavy. Thick, woollen undercoat. Can be any colour except liver or chocolate. **Character:** Lively and good-natured. **Pet Suitability:** Reasonably easy to train. Good guard.

The Tibetan Terrier is a larger cousin of the Tibetan Lhasa Apso which looks more like a miniature Old English Sheepdog than a terrier. It was only recognized as a purebred animal in Britain in the 1930s having previously been classed together with Shih Tzu and the Lhasa Apso as a Lhasa Terrier. Nomads travelling the mountainous country of ancient Tibet used this dog to protect their camps. It was also considered a valuable herding dog and a token of good luck.

THE WORKING ❦ GROUP ❦

Group Features

The Working Group is the largest group, containing those breeds which serve the needs of man such as herding dogs, rescue dogs, tracker dogs, guide dogs and general helpers. Often dogs of this group possess a variety of these skills.

HERDING

Dogs were well-established as human hunting companions by the time man began to domesticate large numbers of other animals such as the horse, cow and sheep around 1000 BC. Farmers, however, had no real use for hunting dogs who might kill their livestock and so herding dogs which could help round up domestic animals without attacking them were developed from the hunting breeds.

• Herding dogs possess a natural instinct to run with other animals, yet neither injure nor kill their quarry.

• Generally speaking, dogs from the herding breeds are more easily trained than those from the hound and terrier groups.

• Shepherds in the past always preferred white sheepdogs since they could be easily distinguished from wolves. Many herding dogs today still retain a great deal of white in their coats.

GUARD DOGS

Dogs have naturally strong protective instincts and have been used for centuries to guard the homestead. Today that role is extended to cover factories and other industrial premises. Some modern specimens, like the Dobermann, were specifically bred as security dogs, but other formidable guard dogs tend to come from the herding and allied breeds. Ancestors of the German Shepherd, a highly popular guard, for example, were once highly–prized pastoral dogs used for herding and farm work.

RESCUE DOGS

The Saint Bernard was a breed developed in the early 18th century by monks in Switzerland who needed dogs that could both guide and rescue people as they journeyed the snow-covered paths. Newfoundlands and German Shepherds also display a similar aptitude for such work.

Bearded Collie

Size: Height 51-56cm/20-22ins, weight 18-27kg/40-60lbs. **Lifespan:** 12-13 years.
Identifying Features: Broad, flat skull. Wide-set, large eyes. Medium-sized, drooping ears. Well-boned legs covered in shaggy hair. Deep chest, well-sprung ribs. Oval feet with well-padded soles. Low-set, well-feathered tail. Soft, furry undercoat, harsh and shaggy topcoat. Colour is any shade of grey, brown, fawn, black and blue, with or without white markings.
Character: Energetic, affectionate and gregarious.
Pet Suitability: Makes a good family pet for people with energy. Needs constant mental and physical stimulation. Coat needs regular attention.

Almost certainly related to the Old English Sheepdog and the Border Collie, the Bearded Collie was used in the past as a hill-gathering sheepdog sent out to round up the widely scattered flocks. Today, its herding instinct is still very strong. It is quite a noisy worker and possesses incredible stamina.

Belgian Shepherd Dog

Four varieties of Belgian Shepherd Dog exist, differing only in coat and colour. For centuries, these dogs herded and guarded sheep in Belgium and they belong to a similar group of European Herding dogs which includes the German Shepherd. Belgian Shepherd Dogs have a more slender build and are shorter in the back and higher in the leg.

Groenendael

Size: Height 56-66cm/22-26ins, weight 27.5-28.5kg/61-63lb. **Lifespan:** 13-14 years.
Identifying Features: Finely-chiselled, long head, muzzle tapering to nose. Slightly almond-shaped eyes surrounded by black rims. Triangular, erect ears set high on head. Very supple, well-muscled neck. Strong-boned forequarters, powerful hindquarters. Deep chest. Rounded feet with springy soles and large, dark claws. Long, straight, medium-harsh black coat, with or without small white markings. **Character:** Vigilant and intelligent, never aggressive.
Pet Suitability: Very strong guarding and herding instincts. Easily trained. Needs plenty of exercise.

The Groenendael is the best-known of the Belgian sheepdogs. It was established from old working stock in 1880 by Nicholas Rose of Groenendael and was recognized properly in Belgium in 1891. These dogs first arrived in Britain from France in 1931 and their popularity rose steadily after the Second World War. Like other Belgian Shepherd Dogs, they are used in Europe as police dogs and also for droving sheep and cattle.

Tervueren

Size: Height 56-66cm/22-26ins, weight 27.5-28.5kg/61-63lb). **Lifespan:** 12-14 years.
Identifying Features: Well-chiselled, long head, muzzle tapering to nose. Slightly almond-shaped eyes surrounded by black rims. Triangular, erect ears set high on head. Very supple, well-muscled neck. Strong-boned forequarters, powerful hindquarters. Deep chest. Rounded feet with springy soles and large, dark claws. Coat is long, straight and abundant forming a ruff around the neck. Shorter hair on head. Colour is any shade of red, fawn or grey with black overlay. **Character:** Alert and very active.
Pet Suitability: Easily trained, but needs firm control. Makes a good watchdog. Requires regular exercise and some grooming.

The Tervueren might be accurately described as a fawn-coloured Groenendael and in many countries they are classed together. The Tervueren has only recently come to Britain, but is increasingly used in Europe as a scent detector, highly competent at sniffing out drugs.

Laekenois

Size: Height 56-66cm/22-26ins, weight 27.5-28.5kg/61-63lb. **Lifespan:** 12-14 years.
Identifying Features: Finely-chiselled, long head, muzzle tapering to nose. Slightly almond-shaped eyes surrounded by black rims. Triangular, erect ears set high on head. Very supple, well-muscled neck. Strong-boned forequarters, powerful hindquarters. Deep chest. Rounded feet with springy soles and large, dark claws. Coat is harsh, dry and wiry. Colour is reddish fawn with black shading on muzzle and tail. **Character:** Alert and very active. **Pet Suitability:** Easily trained. Good with children. Makes an excellent watchdog. Often hostile to other dogs.

The rarest of the four breeds, the Laekenois was first recognized in 1897. It is named after a royal residence of Queen Henrietta of Belgium.

Malinois

Size: Height 56-66cm/22-26ins, weight 27.5-28.5kg/61-63lb. **Lifespan:** 12-14 years. **Identifying Features:** Finely-chiselled, long head, muzzle tapering to nose. Slightly almond-shaped eyes surrounded by black rims. Triangular, erect ears set high on head. Very supple, well-muscled neck. Strong-boned forequarters, powerful hindquarters. Deep chest. Rounded feet with springy soles and large, dark claws. Thick, bushy tail. Coat is short and hard with a woolly undercoat. **Character:** Active and alert. **Pet Suitability:** Strong guarding instinct. Easily trained. Good with children.

The relatively rare Malinois is a short-coated version of the Tervueren usually with a reddish, mahogany colouring although it may also be grey or fawn. Of the four Belgian Shepherd Dogs, it is closest in appearance to the German Shepherd.

Bernese Mountain Dog

Size: Height 58-70cm/23-27.5ins, weight 40-44kg/87-90lb. **Lifespan:** 10-12 years.
Identifying Features: Flat skull with dark brown, almond-shaped eyes. High-set triangular-shaped ears. Strong, muscular neck and body. Broad chest. Short, round feet. Well-feathered tail without curl. Coat is soft and silky, long and slightly wavy. Colour is jet black with rich reddish-brown and white markings.
Character: Good-natured and fearless.
Pet Suitability: Kind and devoted family dog, but needs an experienced handler. Good watchdog. Easily trained.

The Bernese Mountain Dog is the most popular of the Swiss Mountain Dogs which were split into four separate breeds towards the end of the 1800s. All four types are closely linked and were used for herding sheep and cattle, for pulling carts to market, and for guarding property. The Bernese, one of the two largest of the group, is still a working breed, not ideally suited to urban life.

Border Collie

> **Size:** Height 46-54cm/18-21ins, weight
> 14-22kg/30-49lb. **Lifespan:** 12-14 years. **Identifying
> Features:** Coat can be rough or smooth in a wide
> variety of colours, although white markings should
> not be too pronounced. **Character:** High-powered,
> intelligent, working dog. **Pet Suitability:** Not a good
> domestic pet. Demands careful handling and
> plenty of freedom to roam.

The Border Collie, which derives its name from the
border between Scotland and England, was one of
the first Collies to win at the Sheepdog Trials. It is
renowned for its 'strong eye', enabling it to 'hold' a
sheep with its menacing stare until the sheep

stands still
or moves
backwards. It
is expected to
run between
64–80km/
40–50 miles
a day herding
sheep, a task
which calls
for great
stamina.

Bouvier des Flandres

Size: Height 58-69cm/23-27ins, weight 27-40kg/60-88lb. **Lifespan:** 11-12 years. **Identifying Features:** Very thick, abundant topcoat, crisp to the touch. Fine, fluffy undercoat. Coat is dark in colour, ranging from fawn to black and usually brindled or shaded. **Character:** Calm and sensible. **Pet Suitability:** Makes a superb watchdog with proper training. Requires regular grooming and adequate exercise.

The Bouvier des Flandres is a European breed, possibly descended from griffons. Once very popular as a cattle droving dog, its status as a working animal has been somewhat undermined by modern farming methods, but the breed is quite well known nowadays as a show dog, particularly in America and Canada. In some countries these dogs are trained for working trials and police operations. They are relative newcomers to Britain.

Boxer

Size: Height 53-63cm/21-25ins, weight 25-32kg/55-70lb. **Lifespan:** 12 years. **Identifying Features:** Short, glossy coat. Colour can be any shade of fawn and brindle with a dark muzzle. **Character:** Fearless, self-assured and fun-loving. **Pet Suitability:** Ideal dog for energetic, experienced owners. Needs plenty of exercise, but minimal grooming. Gentle with children. Excellent family guard.

The Boxer emerged at the end of the 19th century in Germany. Its exact origins are unclear but it may well be a descendent of the Bullenbeisser, an ancient Mastiff breed, once used for bull-baiting and boar hunting. It is also thought to have received a boost of English Bulldog blood during the final stages of its evolution. The Boxer's vibrant energy has recently been put to good use by police forces and Customs officers throughout Europe, but they are also particularly appealing show dogs.

Briard

Size: Height 57-69cm/23-27ins, weight 33.5-34.5kg/74-76lb. **Lifespan:** 11-13 years. **Identifying Features:** Coat is long and slightly wavy, resembling goat hair to the touch. Colour can be black, slate grey, or fawn with dark shading. **Character:** Very intelligent, fearless and happy. **Pet Suitability:** Energetic, requiring a good deal of vigorous exercise. Coat needs daily grooming. Makes a superb watchdog.

Also known as the Berger de Brie, the Briard is now one of France's most popular companion dogs. Once used as a herding and watchdog, this breed was only introduced into Britain in the 1960s although its popularity has increased rapidly since. It is a strong, muscular animal with a rugged appearance. It moves effortlessly with a surprising turn of speed.

Bullmastiff

Size: Height 64-69cm/25-27ins, weight
41-59kg/90-130lb. **Lifespan:** 10-12 years. **Identifying
Features:** Large, square skull with short muzzle. Broad
nose with wide-sreading nostrils. Medium-sized, dark
eyes separated by a distinct furrow. V-shaped, high-set
ears. Well-arched, very muscular neck. Thick, straight
forelegs and strong, muscular hindlegs. Wide, deep
chest. Cat-like feet. High-set tail, thick at root and
tapering. Coat lies flat to the body and is short and
hard. Colours can be any shade of fawn, brindle or
red, always with a black muzzle. **Character:** Calm,
gentle and protective. **Pet Suitability:** Makes an
excellent companion for children. Can be stubborn
and difficult to train. Minimum grooming required.
Has a large appetite and requires regular exercise.

The Bullmastiff is the only breed of watchdog
specifically created in Britain by crossing the
Mastiff with the Bulldog in the ratio of 60/40. It is one
of the newest breeds only recognized by the British
Kennel Club in 1924, although similar dogs were used a
long time before this by gamekeepers wishing to ward
off poachers. A Bullmastiff could overtake an intruder
and keep them pinned down without ever using its
teeth. The modern Bullmastiff is still very reluctant to
bite unless trained to do so and is a powerful and
dependable animal.

Collie (Rough and Smooth-coated)

> **Size:** Height 51-61cm/20-24ins, weight 18-30kg/40-66lb. **Lifespan:** 12-14 years. **Identifying Features:** Smooth-coats have a short, flat topcoat of a harsh texture with a very dense undercoat. Colour in both varieties is sable, tricolour or blue merle, all usually with white markings. **Character:** Friendly and obedient. **Pet Suitability:** Good watchdog, usually easy to train and very clean. Requires regular exercise. The Rough Collie is particularly gentle and protective of children. It also needs a certain amount of grooming.

Collies probably first arrived in Britain with the Romans and over the years were possibly interbred with the Borzoi, Deerhound and Newfoundland. Today's Rough and Smooth-coated Collies are more immediate relatives of Scottish working collies used by cattle drovers and sheep farmers. The Rough Collie was one of the first breeds to achieve fame as a show dog and was a particular favourite of Queen Victoria. Over the years, the drive and stamina of a working dog has been overridden and the Rough Collie is now primarily an exhibition and companion animal. It has also come to be known as the 'Lassie Collie' because of its association with the MGM cinema star 'Lassie'.

The Smooth-coated Collie, which has never achieved the popularity of the Rough, is the only collie breed without a long coat and is identical to the Rough apart from this feature. Both breeds originally appeared in the same litters however, and were shown in the same classes a century ago.

Dobermann

Size: Height 65-69cm/25.5-27ins, weight
30-40kg/66-88lb. **Lifespan:** 12 years.
Identifying Features: Coat is smooth, short and hard.
Colours are black, brown, blue or fawn, all with tan
markings. **Character:** Intelligent, loyal and obedient.
Pet Suitability: An excellent guard and family
companion if properly trained and firmly controlled.

The Dobermann was created during the 1880s by a
German tax collector, Herr Louis Dobermann, who
wanted a medium-sized watchdog to protect him while
working. He is thought to have used Rottweilers, German
Pinschers, Weimaraners and possibly Manchester Terriers
to produce the breed. Arguably the best guard dog in
existence, the Dobermann is used worldwide by police
and security
firms. A
tough and
formidable
animal, it
will normally
only attack
if provoked.

German Shepherd Dog

Size: Height 55-66cm/22-26ins, weight 34-43kg/75-95lb. **Lifespan:** 12-13 years.
Identifying Features: Straight, hard, close-lying, weather-resistant coat in a variety of colours.
Character: Highly intelligent and responsive.
Pet Suitability: Needs an owner committed to early training. Good watchdog. Requires regular exercise.

Ancestors of the German Shepherd Dog were used to herd and guard sheep for many centuries. During the First World War the Germans trained it as a messenger, and to locate the wounded. Recognizing its worth, soldiers from various allied countries returned home with dogs of this breed. By 1926 its popularity had spread worldwide, but indiscriminate breeding meant

that its reputation suffered some damage. The German Shepherd Dog has since recovered its rightful position as one of the most versatile and popular dogs in the world.

Great Dane

Size: Height 71-76cm/28-30ins, weight
46-54kg/100-120lb. **Lifespan:** 10 years.
Identifying Features: Coat is short, sleek and dense.
Colour is usually fawn, although brindle, blue and
black or harlequin (white with black or blue patches)
also exist. **Character:** Friendly and outgoing.
Pet Suitability: Makes a devoted companion and
guardian, but is an expensive purchase.

Despite its name, the Great Dane has no connection
with Denmark and its ancestry may be traced to
dogs brought to Europe by Scythian tribes in Russia
hundreds of years ago. During the Middle Ages the
German nobility used this large and powerful animal to
hunt wild boar and it is therefore assumed that it was
bred in
Germany for
this purpose.
The Germans
refer to it as
the German
Mastiff, or
simply the
German Dog.

Hungarian Puli

Size: Height 37-44cm/14.5-17.5ins, weight
10-15kg/22-33lb. **Lifespan:** 12-13 years.
Identifying Features: Usually reddish black or grey in
colour. **Character:** Loyal and highly intelligent.
Pet Suitability: Good companion and house guard.
Adapts well to town life. Not suitable for casual dog
owners as the coat needs considerable care.

The Puli is thought to have been introduced to
Hungary by the central Asian Magyar tribes.
Almost certainly an ancestor of the poodle, the dog's
most outstanding feature is its coat which is long and
extremely dense and falls to floor length in narrow cords
when the dog reaches maturity. Outside of Hungary,
where it still enjoys working sheep, the Puli is almost
exclusively known as a show dog, although some have proved successful police dogs.

Maremma Sheepdog

Size: Height 60-73cm/23.5-28.5ins, weight 30-45kg/66-100lb. **Lifespan:** 11-13 years. **Identifying Features:** Harsh, abundant, weather-proof coat forming a thick collar at the neck. Colour is always white. **Character:** Intelligent and lively. **Pet Suitability:** Very much an outdoor type. Strong-willed and often difficult to train. Not good with other dogs.

The Maremma Sheepdog is an extremely hardy Italian herding breed found in the Abruzzi region of central Italy. Obviously related to the French Pyrenean and the Hungarian Kuvasz, it is only recently becoming known outside of its homeland where it was used originally to guard flocks against wolves, bears and human predators. This dog has a strong territorial instinct and makes an excellent guard.

Mastiff

Size: Height (approx.) 70-76cm/27-30ins, weight (approx.) 86-100kg/190-220lb. **Lifespan:** 7-10 years. **Identifying Features:** Short, close-lying coat. Colour is apricot-fawn, silver-fawn or dark fawn-brindle, with black muzzle, nose and ears. **Character:** Good-natured and courageous. **Pet Suitability:** Very effective guard dog. Expensive to keep.

Together with the St Bernard, the Mastiff breed is one of the heaviest in existence. Ancient drawings confirm that a broad-muzzled mastiff type of animal existed in Assyria by about 700 BC. When the Romans arrived in Britain in the first century AD, they found similar dogs and exported them back to Rome for pit-fighting. Later in its history, the Mastiff was used in Britain as a watchdog to protect farms and other property against various predators. As with many of the larger breeds, it is now more popular in America.

Newfoundland

Size: Height 66-71cm/26-28ins, weight 50-68kg/110-150lb. **Lifespan:** 11 years. **Identifying Features:** Double coat, slightly oily and lying flat. Colours can be black with bronze tinges, or chocolate with a white chest, toes and claw tips. **Character:** Very gentle, docile and patient. **Pet Suitability:** Loyal and deeply attached to its owner. Should have access to swimming water and plenty of exercise.

The origins of the Newfoundland are uncertain. Many North Americans claim it as a native breed, while others argue that it descends from Pyrenean Mountain Dogs, brought to America by French fishermen. The breed derives its current name from the island on which the dogs were used for haulage and marine work. It is an excellent, speedy swimmer with a natural life-saving instinct.

Norwegian Buhund

Size: Height 41-46cm/16-18ins, weight 24-26kg/53-58lb. **Lifespan:** 12-15 years. **Identifying Features:** Lean, wedge-shaped head, narrowing towards nose. Dark-brown eyes, with dark eyelids. Erect, pointed ears. Medium length, lean neck. Stocky, compact body with deep chest and strong legs. Rather small, oval feet. High-set tail, tightly curled and carried over the back. Colour is wheaten, red or black, with black on the muzzle and ears. **Character:** Fearless and energetic. **Pet Suitability:** Makes an excellent companion and is good with children. Easy to train and a good watchdog.

The Norwegian Buhund is believed to have sailed with the Vikings and almost certainly accompanied its Norwegian masters to Iceland when they invaded in AD874. Later on, the Norwegian Buhund was used as an all-round working dog on the remoter farms of Norway where its strong herding instinct was put to good use. This dog thrives on physical exercise and has more recently been successfully trained as a sheepdog in Australia.

Old English Sheepdog

Size: Height 56-61cm/22-24ins, weight 29.5-30.5kg/65-67lb. **Lifespan:** 12-13 years. **Identifying Features:** Rather square head with truncated muzzle. Wide-set, dark eyes. Small ears carried flat to side of head. Long, strong, gracefully arched neck. Well-boned, perfectly straight forelegs. Broad, muscular loins. Stands lower at shoulder than at the loins. Small, round feet with thick pads. Coat is abundant, shaggy and waterproof. Tail is always docked extremely short, giving it the name 'Bobtail'. Colour is any shade of grey, grizzle or blue, with or without white markings. **Character:** Intelligent, steady and sensible. **Pet Suitability:** Thrives on affection and human companionship. Gentle with children. Makes an excellent guard. Profuse coat demands extensive grooming.

The Old English Sheepdog is probably a descendent of the Bearded Collie and other foreign breeds such as the Briard. It was used by shepherds in the past to guard flocks of 'folded' sheep kept in makeshift enclosures and moved to fresh ground each day. For this type of work, the dog had to be 'close-run' and noisy, a driver rather than a herder. It has become a hugely popular breed today, particularly in America. It is a home-loving animal, although many of the breed have found their way into the hands of totally unsuitable owners, ill-prepared to care for such large dogs.

Pyrenean Mountain Dog

Size: Height 65-81cm/26-32ins, weight
45-60kg/99-132lb. **Lifespan:** 11-12 years.
Identifying Features: Coat is profuse, with a fine
undercoat and a thick, slightly wavy topcoat. Colour
is mainly white, with or without patches of badger,
grey or lemon. **Character:** Intelligent and quite
independent. **Pet Suitability:** Gentle, affectionate and
tolerant, especially with children, but possesses a
strong territorial instinct.

The Pyrenean Mountain Dog is probably related to
the Italian Maremma, Hungarian Kuvasz and
Turkish Karabash and is found on both the Spanish and
the French side of the Pyrénées. It is one of a number of
giant breeds bred in Europe centuries ago to guard flocks
at up to 1500m/5000ft above sea level. Although almost
extinct at the
turn of the
century, these
dogs are now
quite popular
in Britain as
well as in
America,
where they are
known as the
Great
Pyrénées.

Rottweiler

Size: Height 58-69cm/23-27ins, weight 41-50kg/90-110lb. **Lifespan:** 11-12 years.
Identifying Features: Coat is flat and course, with an invisible undercoat. Colour is always black with clearly defined rich tan or mahogany brown markings.
Character: Self-assured, with a natural guarding instinct, not aggressive or vicious by nature.
Pet Suitability: Happy to live in either town or city.

The Rottweiler is an ancient breed which may have travelled to Germany with the Roman legions. During the Middle Ages it was prized by the nobility as a boarhunting dog. The modern version was bred in Rottweil, south Germany in the 1800s as a cattle drover and watchdog. Today, the Rottweiler is popular throughout the world and has proven itself a good, all-round family pet and an excellent guard dog if handled by owners with some experience.

St Bernard

Size: Height 61-71cm/24-28ins, weight 50-91kg/110-200lb. **Lifespan:** 11 years. **Identifying Features:** Massive skull with short muzzle. Large, black nose. Dark-brown eyes. Heavy-boned legs of good length. Wide, deep chest. Medium sized ears, lying close to cheeks. Long, thick and muscular neck. Large, compact feet. High-set tail should not curl over back. Two coat types, Rough coats and Smooth coats. Rough is dense flat, fuller round neck and thighs with well-feathered tail. Smooth is close with only slight feathering on tail and thighs. Colour is usually orange, mahogany-brindle or red-brindle with white markings.
Character: Tender, trustworthy and intelligent.
Pet Suitability: Very large dog whose lifestyle demands both space and money. Loyal and benevolent, especially gentle with children. Careful feeding required.

Originally descended from the alpine mastiffs kept as watchdogs and pathfinders by monks of the St Bernard Hospice in the Swiss Alps, the St Bernard has since been revitalized with Newfoundland blood to improve stamina. Few can afford to keep a St Bernard today, or to care for it properly in a city or town environment. America, however, has always shown a keen interest in giant breeds and the St Bernard is now more popular there today than in its original European home. Movement should always be smooth and free-flowing despite the animal's great bulk.

Samoyed

Size: Height 46-56cm/18-22ins, weight
23-30kg/50-66lb. **Lifespan:** 12 years.
Identifying Features: Double coat with a harsh,
weather-resistant, stand-off topcoat and a soft, dense
undercoat. Colour is pure white or cream.
Character: Affectionate and very fond of human
companionship. **Pet Suitability:** Needs a very
experienced owner with patience to train it. Requires
lots of exercise and grooming.

The Samoyed derives its name from a nomadic
people living in central Asia who held it in great
esteem and used it for herding reindeer, guarding tents
and pulling sledges. This dog also possessed a good nose
for tracking and a powerful hunting instinct. Several
Arctic explorers have chosen to take a Samoyed on polar
expeditions since it has a reputation for longevity and is
energetic, hardy
and a determined
companion. A
unique feature of
the coat is
its smiling
expression, the
result of its black
upward-curling
lips.

Shetland Sheepdog

Size: Height 35-37cm/14-15ins, weight 6-7kg/14-16lb. **Lifespan:** 12-14 years.
Identifying Features: Profuse coat with a luxurious mane and frill. Colour is sable, tricolour, blue-merle, black and white, or black and tan.
Character: Sweet-tempered, sensitive dogs.
Pet Suitability: Makes a good family pet, very clean and intelligent. Suitable for both urban and country life.

A smaller version of the earlier working sheepdogs used off Scotland's north coast for keeping sheep, ponies and hens under control, the Shetland Sheepdog looks rather like a miniature Rough Collie. Now rarely used as a sheep-herding animal, it is a very popular miniature breed in Japan and is becoming increasingly popular in Great Britain as a companion animal.

Siberian Husky

Size: Height 51-60cm/20-23.5ins, weight 16-27kg/35-60lb. **Lifespan:** 11-13 years. **Identifying Features:** The double coat is dense and medium in length. Can be any colour, usually with black markings on the head. **Character:** Loyal, alert and very willing to learn. **Pet Suitability:** Makes a good companion for those living in the countryside.

The Siberian Husky was once the exclusive property of the Chukchi nomads who used it to pull sled and herd reindeer in the tundra regions of north-east Asia. During the 19th century fur-traders and gold-diggers travelling to Asia from America and Canada brought

these animals back to their homeland. The American Kennel Club recognized the breed in 1930 and its popularity as a pet, show dog and racing dog has increased since. A lesser number of this breed made their way to Britain, where owners are keen to maintain their working instincts.

Swedish Vallhund

Size: Height 31-35cm/12-14ins, weight
11-15kg/25-35lb. **Lifespan:** 12-14 years. **Identifying
Features:** Hard, dense, medium-length topcoat with a
soft, woolly undercoat. Colour is usually grey,
grey-brown, red-brown or red- yellow with white
markings. **Character:** Friendly, energetic and eager to
please. **Pet Suitability:** An excellent worker and
efficient guard.

It has been suggested that the Swedish Vallhund,
which closely resembles a Pembroke Corgi, was taken
from Wales to Scandinavia by the Vikings. In Sweden it
was used as a multi-purpose farm dog, expected to herd
animals, keep a watchful eye on property and control
rodents. Its diminishing numbers went almost unnoticed
until the late 1940s when the breed was revived by a

Swedish breeder,
von Rosen. It is
now relatively
popular as a
companion and
as an exhibition
animal.

Welsh Corgi (Cardigan)

Size: Height 27-32cm/10.5-12.5ins, weight 11-17kg/25-38lb. **Lifespan:** 12-14 years. **Identifying Features:** Fox-like head. Wide-set, dark eyes. Large, erect ears with slightly rounded tips. Muscular, well-developed neck. Short, strong-boned legs. Fairly long body with prominent chest bone. Rather large, round feet. Fox-like brush tail carried low. Coat is short and hard-textured. Can be any colour with or without white markings. **Character:** Alert, active and intelligent. **Pet Suitability:** A robust working dog. Not good with children; has a marked tendency to snap. Not easily trained and not good with other dogs. Makes an excellent watchdog.

Welsh Corgi (Pembroke)

Size: Height 25-31cm/10-12ins, weight 10-12kg/20-26lb. **Lifespan:** 12-14 years. **Identifying Features:** Fox-shaped head. Round, brown, slightly oblique eyes. Pricked, medium-sized ears. Short, ample-boned legs. Shorter-length body than Cardigan with broad, deep chest. Short tail. Straight, medium length topcoat with dense undercoat. Colour is usually red, sable, fawn, or black and tan, with or without white markings. **Character:** Outgoing and workmanlike. **Pet Suitability:** Not good with children. Not easily trained and not good with other dogs. An excellent watchdog.

Two types of Welsh Corgi exist: the Pembroke Corgi and the Cardigan Corgi. Both are often referred to as 'heelers' and were originally bred as herding dogs, with a particular skill for droving cattle. The Pembroke is the smaller of the two breeds and usually has its tail docked. The two were only separated in 1934 and the Pembroke became far more popular as a result of royal patronage. Nowadays, the Pembroke is a much heavier and less agile dog that would experience some difficulty performing its original duties. The Cardigan is long in proportion to its height, with larger ears and slightly bowed forelegs.

THE
~ TOY GROUP ~

Group Features

Toy dogs were first created over 2000 years ago in Europe and also at roughly the same time in the Far East. They were specifically bred as pets and human companions and most are related to larger breeds in other groups. In spite of their size, these are very robust dogs, and if properly cared for are just as healthy, active and formidable as their standard-sized relatives.

• The Romans may have been the first to breed miniature dogs in the West. The small white Maltese is generally thought to be of Roman origin.

• The Pekingese, or Lion Dog of Peking, is said to have the most ancient lineage of all Eastern toy breeds. It was first bred to reflect the lion spirit of Buddha. Later, it became a great favourite at the Chinese imperial court, encouraging the fashion for miniature, snub-nosed breeds.

• From the Renaissance onward, toy dogs were a symbol of luxury for the European aristocracy, eventually becoming popular at various European courts. Several important people had portraits painted with their dogs.

• The famous artists Veronese, Reubens and Rembrandt, all included Papillons in their paintings.

- The King Charles Spaniel first arrived in Britain from France in the 16th century and was a highly popular breed with King Charles II.
- Queen Victoria and Mozart were also very attached to their toy Pomeranians.
- The famous 18th–century English artist, Thomas Gainsborough, painted his Pomeranian with her puppy.

Affenpinscher

Size: Height 25-30cm/10-12ins, weight 3-3.5kg/7-8lb. **Lifespan:** 14-15 years. **Identifying Features:** Rough coat, harsh in texture, longer on shoulders, neck and head. Colour is usually black. **Character:** Loyal and affectionate. **Pet Suitability:** Lively and spirited. Not easy to train and has a tendency to snap. Good watchdog. Requires only moderate exercise.

One of the sturdier breeds of Toy Dogs, the Affenpinscher originated in Germany where its name means 'Monkey Terrier'. It is thought that the ancestors of these dogs may have included local pinschers and pug-like breeds from Asia. At one time both popular and formidable ratting terriers full of energy and confidence, the Affenpinscher is now quite rare in its native land and is most common in the north of America

Bichon Frisé

Size: Height 23-30cm/9-11ins, weight 3-6kg/7-12lb.
Lifespan: 14 years. **Identifying Features:** Slightly
rounded skull. Black, button-shaped eyes. Large, black
nose. Loose-hanging ears, slightly higher than eye level.
Fairly long, arched neck. Straight legs, broad thighs.
Well-developed forechest. Round, well-knuckled feet
with black nails. Tail curved gracefully over the back,
never docked. Fine, silky coat with soft corkscrew
curls. Colour is always white.**Character:** Friendly
and outgoing. **Pet Suitability:** Ideal for most
households; thrives on human companionship.
Easily trained, good with children and other dogs.
Regular grooming is essential.

The exact origins of the
Bichon Frisé are unclear.
It has been suggested that
the Spaniards introduced it
to the Canary Islands and
that in the 14th century
Italian sailors re-discovered it
and brought it back to Europe
where it quickly became a royal
favourite. 'Bichon' is French for lap
dog and this animal has always been
bred as a pet. It was only recognized
by the British and American
Kennel Clubs in the 1970s.

Cavalier King Charles Spaniel

Size: Height 31-33cm/12-13ins, weight 5-8kg/10-18lb. **Lifespan:** 9-14 years. **Identifying Features:** Skull almost flat between the ears with shallow stop. Large, dark, round eyes. High-set, well-feathered long ears. Compact, cushioned feet. Tail occasionally docked. Coat is long and silky, free from curl but with plenty of feathering. Colour is black and tan, tricolour, ruby (red chestnut), or Blenheim (chestnut and white). **Character:** Affectionate and fearless. **Pet Suitability:** An excellent family dog. Undemanding and easy to train. Good with children and older people. Some grooming needed. Line should be checked for inherited heart disease.

The Cavalier King Charles Spaniel is much more popular nowadays than the King Charles Spaniel with whom it shares a common ancestry. Spaniels with the longer, more tapered muzzle and flat skull were a favourite of King Charles II but by the 1800s a shorter-faced, snub-nosed dog began to appear. In the 1920s however, a prize was offered at Cruft's Dog Show in London to anyone who could produce a dog resembling the earlier King Charles Spaniel. The Cavalier King Charles Spaniel was re-established as a result.

Chihuahua

Size: Height 15-23cm/6-9ins, weight 1-3kg/2-6lb.
Lifespan: 12-14 years. **Identifying Features:** Two coat types. Long Coat has a soft textured covering of hair with fully plumed tail. Short Coat hair is also soft in texture, but close and glossy. Coat is any colour or mixture of colours. **Character:** Spirited, intelligent and even-tempered. **Pet Suitability:** Adores human companionship, but needs careful handling because of its fragile frame. Should not be kept in a hectic household or one with small children.

Generally accepted as one of the smallest breeds of dogs in the world, the Chihuahua is said to derive its name from the Mexican state from which it was first exported to the United States in the mid-19th century. The original dog was larger and tougher than the modern variety and was probably descended from a combination of small dogs found in Texas, Arizona and Mexico.

Chinese Crested Dog

Size: Height 23-33cm/9-13ins, weight
2-5.5kg/5-12lb. **Lifespan:** 12-13 years.
Identifying Features: Hairless dogs have soft, smooth
skin with a plume on the head and hairy feet and tail.
Powderpuff puppies are covered with very fine long
hair which they retain in adulthood. Can be any
colour or combination of colours. **Character:** A happy,
intelligent dog. **Pet Suitability:** Affectionate family
pet. Very active with strong protective instincts.

The Chinese Crested Dog is now extinct in China.
Its history remains mysterious with various
countries claiming a role in its origin and
development. Some
believe it was
kept by the
Chinese
Mandarins as a
pet, others
suggest it was
bred in Africa
and eventually
brought to South
America by the
Toltecs. Hairless dogs are
the result of a defective
gene.

English Toy Terrier

> **Size:** Height 25-30cm/10-12ins, weight 3-4kg/6-8lb.
> **Lifespan:** 12-13 years. **Identifying Features:** Coat is
> sleek and glossy with rich tan markings that must
> follow a clearly defined pattern. **Character:** Warm,
> affectionate nature, although naturally suspicious of
> strangers. **Pet Suitability:** Alert and lively. A
> convenient size for urban life. Good watchdog.

A sturdy, sporty dog, the English Toy Terrier is descended from the Manchester Terrier and at the end of the last century was known by a variety of names including Toy Manchester Terrier, Toy Black and Tan and Miniature Black and Tan. The breed is an old one, most famous in the past for its impressive performances in the rat pits. This dog still retains its sporting instincts but is now relatively rare.

Griffon Bruxellois

Size: Height 18-20cm/7-8ins, weight
2.5-5.5kg/6-12lb. **Lifespan:** 12-14 years.
Identifying Features: Two coat types. Rough coat is
harsh and wiry. Smooth coat is short and tight.
Colour is either solid red, black, or black and tan.
Character: Highly intelligent, fun-loving little dog.
Pet Suitability: Easy to train, reliable and watchful
companion with a terrier-like personality.

The Griffon Bruxellois was developed in the late
19th century from a mixture of German
Affenpinscher, Chinese Pug, Belgian street dog and
Yorkshire terrier. Often described as a monkey-dog, it
was originally used to control vermin and was also
regularly seen in the Belgian streets accompanying the
drivers of hansom cabs. Puppies born with the Pug
smooth coat have been named Petit Brabançon.

Italian Greyhound

Size: Height 33-38cm/13-15ins, weight 3-3.5kg/7-8lb. **Lifespan:** 13-14 years. **Identifying Features:** Short, fine and glossy coat. Colour is black, fawn, red, cream and blue, with or without broken white. **Character:** Intelligent and good-natured. **Pet Suitability:** A comfort-loving animal that makes a good family pet. Susceptible to cold and wet but minimum grooming required. Strong sporting streak and impressive turn of speed.

The smallest of the sighthound family, the Italian Greyhound is a very ancient breed possibly created from the standard-sized Greyhound. It was probably taken by the Romans from Egypt to the Mediterranean some time in the 6th Century BC, and has been extremely popular in various European courts over the centuries.

Japanese Chin

Size: Height 23-25cm/9-10ins, weight 2-5kg/4-11lb.
Lifespan: 12 years. **Identifying Features:** Profuse, silky coat with pronounced ruff and feathering on the legs, feet and tail. Colour is predominantly white with either black or red markings.
Character: Intelligent, self-assured and fun-loving.
Pet Suitability: Good house dog with a deep bark for its size. Sociable with other dogs.

The exact origin of the dainty Japanese Chin is uncertain but it is obviously related to the Pekingese and other flat-faced oriental breeds. Thought to have been introduced to Japan by Buddhist monks as early as AD520 the Chin became the cherished companion of the Japanese nobility. It was brought to Europe by

Portugese sailors in the 1600s and in time became a particular favourite of Western royals such as the Queen Victoria.

King Charles Spaniel

Size: Height 25-27cm/10-11ins, weight 4-6kg/8-14lb.
Lifespan: 12 years. **Identifying Features:** Coat is long
and often extremely wavy, never curly. May be
tricolour, black and tan, whole-coloured red, or
Blenheim (pearly white with chestnut red patches).
Character: Cheerful, intelligent and affectionate.
Pet Suitability: Excellent pet. Only a minimum
amount of exercise required.

The King Charles Spaniel is a compact little dog with
a larger head and a less tapered muzzle than its
close relative, the Cavalier. Known as the English Toy
Spaniel in America, it was at one time the most popular
Toy Spaniel in Britain but has now been overtaken by
the Cavalier. The Japanese Chin may be part of its
ancestry also,
since the white
blaze of colour
on the
forehead with
a red dot in
the middle
appears in
both breeds
and is a
highly-prized
feature.

Lowchen

Size: Height 25-33cm/10-13ins, weight 4-8kg/9-18lb.
Lifespan: 12-14 years. **Identifying Features:** Thick,
long silky textured coat, wavy but not curly. Can be
any colour. **Character:** Good-natured and lively.
Pet Suitability: Can be strong-willed and difficult to
train. Good with children, but may challenge other dogs.

The Lowchen won its European name of Petit Chien
Lion because of the way its coat was clipped to
resemble that of a lion. An ancient breed, probably
related to the small barbets or water spaniel and to the
Bichon family, the modern Lowchen was first registered
as a Toy Dog in Britain in 1971, but it is still unknown
in America. The clipped body hair is often a different
shade from the longer areas providing an attractive
contrast of colours.

Maltese

Size: Height 20-25cm/8-10ins, weight 2-3kg/4-6lb.
Lifespan: 14-15 years. **Identifying Features:** Coat is straight, silky and trails on the ground. Colour is always pure white with a hint of lemon. **Character:** Sweet-tempered and lively. **Pet Suitability:** Perfect human companions and excellent, if time-consuming, pet. Very gentle with children and good with other dogs.

The Maltese is known to have existed for more than 2000 years and images of similar dogs have appeared in Egyptian tombs. It is still a subject of debate however, whether the breed originated in Malta or Melita in Sicily. It probably first arrived in Britain with the Romans. The Maltese is distinguished by its soft-textured coat which requires daily grooming and frequent bathing in a mild shampoo.

Miniature Pinscher

Size: Height 25-30cm/10-12ins, weight 4-6kg/8-10lb.
Lifespan: 13-14 years. **Identifying Features:** Very
high-pitched screaming bark. Short, glossy, dense coat,
usually black and tan, solid red, blue or chocolate
in colour. **Character:** Spirited and alert.
Pet Suitability: Good companion; proud and
intelligent. Requires regular exercise, but minimum
grooming. Not good with other dogs.

The Small Pinscher has
been known in Germany
as far back as 16th century,
but the Miniature Pinscher is
often wrongly described as a
miniature Doberman Pinscher,
even though the Doberman was
not produced until the 1870s.
The dog bears a striking
resemblance to the English
Toy Terrier and was originally
used for hunting, chasing and
killing vermin. The modern
Miniature Pinscher is a very
smart-looking dog, influenced
by a number of other breeds
including the Dachshund and
possibly the Italian Greyhound.

Papillon

Size: Height 20-28cm/8-11ins, weight
4-4.5kg/9-10lb. **Lifespan:** 13-15 years. **Identifying
Features:** Moderately long, silky coat, falling flat on
the body but forming a ruff on the chest and ears.
Hair is white with patches of any colour except liver.
Character: Highly intelligent, friendly and playful. **Pet
Suitability:** Excellent pet, easily trained and extremely
protective. Coat needs regular attention.

Papillon is the French word for butterfly, a name
which epitomizes the dramatic shape and position of
the ears on this breed. A narrow white blaze down the
centre of the head also resembles the body of a butterfly.
The breed has two types, one with erect ears, the other
with dropped
ears, known as
Phalène
(meaning
moth). Since
the Renaissance
these dogs have
been very
popular serving
as models for
such painters as
as Rembrandt.

Pekingese

Size: Height 15-23cm/6-9ins, weight 3-6kg/7-12lb.
Lifespan: 12-13 years. **Identifying Features:** Coat is
abundant with long feathering on the ears, legs and
tail. Can be any colour. **Character:** Loyal, stubborn,
sometimes aloof. **Pet Suitability:** Needs a lot of
grooming and careful cleaning of the eyes and
wrinkled face. Not easy to train.

Now a favourite Western breed, the Pekingese is
practically extinct in its native China although at
one point it was bred exclusively at the royal courts of
the Chinese Emperors. In 1860, five Pekes were
captured by British troops and transported back to
Britain where one was immediately presented to Queen

Victoria.
Such royal
patronage
contributed
hugely to the
breed's
popularity
with the
result that
more dogs
were
imported in
due course.

Pomeranian

Size: Height 22-28cm/8.5-11ins, weight 2-3kg/4-5.5lb. **Lifespan:** 15 years. **Identifying Features:** Outer coat is thick and stand-off, undercoat is soft and fluffy. Can be any colour without black or white shading. **Character:** Active, gay and affectionate. **Pet Suitability:** Keen watchdog. Good with children. Daily grooming is essential.

The Pomeranian is the smallest of the spitz breeds and takes its name from its place of origin in the Baltics. The dog which first reached Britain in the 18th century was much larger than its modern relatives, weighing up to 15kg/33lb. When Queen Victoria took an interest in it a century later, the size had been reduced by half. The modern Pomeranian is bred for its smallness, but it still has the temperament of a much larger dog.

Pug

Size: Height 25-28cm/10-11ins, weight 6-8kg/14-18lb. **Lifespan:** 13-15 years.
Identifying Features: Fine, glossy coat. Colour can be silver, apricot, fawn or black with a black mask and ears and a black trace mark running down the back.
Character: Charming, intelligent and tolerant.
Pet Suitability: Affectionate towards children, although strong-willed and not easy to train. Good watchdog. Little grooming or exercise needed, but careful feeding is required.

Ancestors of the Pug lived in the Far East well over 2000 years ago and were originally kept by Buddhist monks. The dog is believed to have first arrived in Europe via the trading ships of the Dutch East India Company in the 16th century. From here, it travelled to Britain with the court of William of Orange. By the 18th century it had became a highly-prized fashion accessory, among royalty and the aristocracy. It is still a very popular companion today and makes a good family pet.

Yorkshire Terrier

Size: Height 22.5-23.5cm/9ins, weight
2.5-3.5kg/5-7lb. **Lifespan:** 14 years.
Identifying Features: Small, narrow head. Dark,
sparkling eyes. Small, V-shaped ears, carried erect.
Straight legs, well covered with hair. Small, round feet
with black nails. Tail usually docked. Perfectly straight
coat of a silky texture. Colouring is steel blue and rich
tan in show dogs, black markings on pet Yorkies never
turn blue. **Character:** Spirited, but even-tempered.
Pet Suitability: Conveniently-sized, popular urban
pet. Good guarding instincts, but not easy to train.
Coat needs regular attention.

The Yorkshire Terrier was bred in the mid-19th
century in the north of England where miners
required a small, yet sturdy terrier to keep down the
numbers of rats underground. This early dog was
eventually refined by breeders to produce a smaller,
prettier animal which was more a fashion accessory than
a worker. Pet and exhibition varieties now exist. The
show dog has long, silky hair sweeping the ground
which needs regular brushing, bathing and oiling. The
hair is then divided up and rolled up into small bundles
to prevent matting. The larger pet Yorkie looks more
like the original breed and is a good sporting
companion. Its coat is often trimmed to a manageable
length.

≈ COMPENDIUM ≈

Classification

Before the first dog show in Britain in the mid-19th century, there were hundreds of variations in the sizes, shapes and colours of dogs within a single breed. Conflicting opinion on how a particular type of dog should look led to the establishment of canine societies and kennel clubs which set out to fix an official 'standard' or ideal by which a dog might be classified.

FUNCTIONS OF THE BRITISH KENNEL CLUB

- To promote in every way the general improvement of dogs.
- To license and control dog shows, field trials, working trials and obedience trials.
- To classify breeds.
- To register and license breed clubs, canine societies and dog–training societies.
- To register pedigree dogs.
- To oversee transfer of ownership.
- To devise and enforce Kennel Club rules.
- To present awards.

The Kennel Club, founded in 1873, took charge of amalgamating all the standards set by individual breed societies throughout the country. The attempt to weed out undesirable characteristics in a given breed resulted in a lengthy description for each type of dog with the emphasis on appearance rather than working ability.

Originally, all dogs were shown together, but the Kennel Club soon set out to link dogs of similar purpose broadly within individual groups, resulting initially in just two categories: sporting and non-sporting. After this, a further subdivision occurred within the sporting group and it was divided into three

groups: Gundogs, Hounds and Terriers. Non-sporting dogs needed further classification also, but this was a slightly more difficult task. Eventually, Toy Dogs were separated out, followed by Working Dogs, and the miscellaneous breeds which remained were labelled Utility Dogs.

The Kennel Club in Britain today has breed standards for six main groups: The Hound Group, Gundog Group, Terrier Group, Utility Group, Working Group and Toy Group.

In America, however, Gundogs are still known as 'Sporting Dogs' and Utility Dogs as 'Non-sporting Dogs'.

Breeding

Dog breeding probably began shortly after the domestication of the dog, somewhere between 10,000 and 35,000 years ago. Man first made use of dogs for hunting and killing other animals before he domesticated them, and having realized their usefulness, he no doubt began to breed them selectively from the best stock. An instinct may be strengthened or weakened by selective breeding and as time went on this shaped dogs for particular tasks, including guarding, rescuing, sledge-pulling, firearm hunting, or simple human companionship. Today, most pedigree dogs are bred to Kennel Club rather than working standards.

Breeding your own dog can be a very rewarding experience, but should not be undertaken lightly; many breeds have inherited problems and it is wrong to embark on breeding pedigree dogs without an understanding of these. If you set out to breed for financial profit, it is unlikely that you'll succeed. Veterinary bills, feeding bills and the sheer amount of time and commitment involved should all be taken into consideration.

BEFORE BREEDING

Breeding should not be undertaken without the advice of an expert. Most pets should be neutered.

• Wait until the bitch is fully mature, usually after she has reached twelve months of age.

• Arrange booster vaccinations for your bitch before she is due to conceive and worm her a week before mating.

Regular Healthcare

Your dog will need to make regular visits to a vet during its lifetime and it is advisable that it has a thorough veterinary examination once a year, usually when receiving its annual vaccination booster. Older dogs will require more regular examination. Often it is best to select a vet who has been recommended by a friend. Many people choose to take out pet health insurance to cover the cost of these visits and to cope with the expensive treatment of unexpected injury or chronic illness.

HEALTH AND SAFETY CHECKS

• Your dog should be wormed every three months. Your vet will prescribe the appropriate wormer.
• Preventative vaccination against contagious diseases such as distemper, hepatitis and leptospirosis is extremely important for your puppy and should be administered as soon as possible. (Check with your vet when this should be but it is usually when the puppy is around eight weeks old.)
• Routinely check your dog at home for discharge from the ears and eyes. Also check the mouth and skin for inflammation and the coat for unwelcome parasites such as fleas.
• Keep toxic substances such as household cleaning solutions out of your dog's reach. Some plants and flowers may also be toxic. Keep easy-to-chew electric cables out of the reach of puppies and younger dogs.

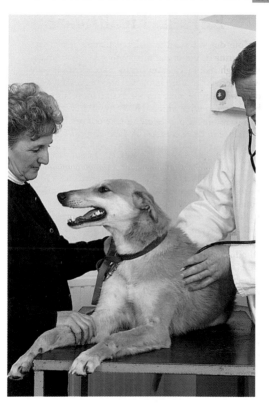

Basic First Aid Procedures

TRAFFIC ACCIDENT

• This is probably the most common cause of serious injury to a dog.

• Approach the dog with caution, it may react aggressively because of the pain.

• Move the dog as little as possible, but if you must move it, it is probably best to use a blanket, sliding it gently underneath the dog. Seek the assistance of another person and lift the dog gently to safety.

• Check for heartbeat and any haemorrhaging. Attempt to stem excessive bleeding by holding a clean pad or clean handkerchief over the wound, binding it tightly with a makeshift bandage.

• Call the nearest vet's surgery to warn of your arrival.

BURNS

• The only recommended first aid is to clean off the offending substance and immerse the body part under cold running water for as long as possible. Seek professional advice immediately.

HEAT STROKE

• This occurs most commonly when a dog has been left in a car on a hot day without ventilation.

• If your dog has not already collapsed it may be panting, vomiting or frothing at the mouth.

• Remove froth and lower the dog's temperature as soon as possible by placing or dousing the animal in cold water.

• Take the dog to the vet immediately where it will be treated with drugs and more cold water.

POISONING

• Signs of poisoning may include collapse, muscular twitching, vomiting, bleeding or convulsions.

• Do not hesitate to contact the vet. Take some of the noxious substance to the vet with you if you know what it is.

• If the dog has only recently swallowed the poison, try to make it vomit. Salt and mustard in water will usually work quickly, or a small piece of washing soda (sodium carbonate) pushed down the throat.

DROWNING

• It is a popular misconception that all dogs can swim, but this is not always the case.

• You must attempt to empty the dog's lungs of water as soon as possible.

• Place the dog's head lower than its body, open its mouth and begin to pump the chest by pressing down on the ribs and releasing the pressure immediately. Repeat at five–second intervals.

CHOKING

• Sometimes a piece of stick, bone or small rubber ball may get stuck in a dog's throat. Your dog may be unable to breathe as a result and swift action is necessary.

• Open the dog's mouth carefully and see if you can remove the object.

• Pumping the chest, as in the case of a drowning dog (see above), may dislodge the foreign body.

• Get your dog to the vet as soon as possible where the object can be removed under anaesthetic.

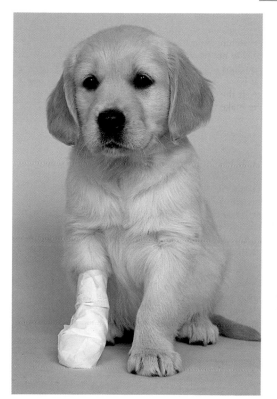

Famous Dogs:

Dogs in Antiquity

The dog's initially perfunctory relationship with the human pack gradually led to a closer bond and certainly by 3000 BC the dog's role had been dramatically transformed. Archaeologists have supplied us with pottery, fossils, wall-paintings and ancient manuscripts which highlight the growing importance of the dog within civilized society, while revealing at the same time that dogs had evolved to such a high degree, they were treated in many cultures as objects of worship.

• The Egyptians entrusted to the dog deity Anubis the responsibility of accompanying their souls to final judgement.

• The Romans made sacrifices to the god Procyon, represented by the constellation *Canis Minor.*

• Ancient Chinese writings which date back to 2000 BC, stress the importance of dogs as sacred animals, bringing happiness and good fortune. Tibetan monks later revered their dogs as canine representations of Buddha.

• One of the seven sacred books of the ancient Persian Zoroastrian religion *Zend Avesta* is given over to the praise and description of dogs. The founder of Zoroastrianism was Zarathustra who was devoted to dogs, their breeding and care.

Dogs in Art

Artists have never tired of paying tribute to the unique importance of the dog and it has been a constant source of artistic inspiration since ancient times.

ARTEFACTS

• The Celts produced these famous Basse-Yutz drinking flagons (c. 400 BC) decorated with two hounds chasing a duck.

• The Romans gave us a number of mosaics featuring the dog. The *Cave canem* ' Beware of the dog' mosaic (c. 400 AD) is perhaps the most famous.

DOGS ON CANVAS

• The 19th century novelist, Emily Brontë, was extremely devoted to her Bullmastiff, 'Keeper' and painted her dog in watercolour.

• The Victorian painter Edwin Landseer frequently depicted the dog in a realistic, anecdotal style.

• Crossbreeds have also been a favourite subject for painters, for example the French artist Constantin Magnier who produced his *L'Ami des Bêtes* in 1910, depicting an old tramp surrounded by a host of faithful mongrels.

• George Stubbs (1724–1806) and Thomas Gainsborough (1727–88) were known particularly for their dog portraiture.

• Impressionists like Renoir and Degas included dogs in their work, both as central figures and as companions to portrait subjects.

Dogs in Literature

MYTHS & LEGENDS

• One of the most famous dogs in Greek mythology is Odysseus's dog, Argos. When Odysseus returned home after twenty years in the Trojan war, his faithful dog ran forward to greet him. Not yet ready to reveal his identity, Odysseus was forced to ignore his pet who died instantly of a broken heart.

• Other ancient Greek canines include Cerberus, the three-headed mastiff-type dog guarding the entrance to Hades, the mythological realm of the dead.

• The King Arthur cycle of tales in English mythology includes references to his dog, Cavall, which left its footprints in stone in Wales.

• The legendary Prince of Wales, Llewellyn, also kept a faithful hound, Gelert, which he killed with his own sword, believing the dog had attacked and murdered his infant son.

• The war-hero Cuchulainn in ancient Celtic mythology whose name means 'hound of Culann' earned his name by slaying a giant watchdog.

DOGS IN FICTION

• For centuries, both adults and children have enjoyed reading various adaptations of *Aesop's Fables,* thought to have been written in the 6th century BC, and containing a number of animal stories featuring dogs.

• Shakespeare made numerous references to dogs in his plays. They are mentioned, for example, in *Twelfth*

Night, Macbeth, and *Two Gentlemen of Verona.*

• During the early 19th century, Sir Walter Scott created his fictional character Dandie Dinmont, a Liddesdale farmer, named after the pack of pepper-coloured terriers he kept. Scott wrote of these dogs: 'They fear nothing that ever cam wi' a hairy skin on't'.

• A century later, J. M. Barrie created 'Nana' the Newfoundland in his children's novel *Peter Pan.*

Dogs on Film

The modern media of television and cinema have helped to immortalize many different dogs and have directly increased the popularity of certain breeds. From the earliest days of Hollywood, producers and directors have recognized the strong public appeal dogs possess, and a very lucrative industry has developed around them as a result. They have been the stars of comedy, adventure, murder-mystery and feature-length animated films.

• The Rough Collie known as 'Lassie' became an international screen star in the 1940s.

• Snoopy, the world's most famous cartoon dog created by David Schulz, who appears both on television and in newspapers internationally, is a type of beagle.

• The Walt Disney Film *Lady and the Tramp* features a gentlemanly Scottish Terrier. Other Walt Disney films devoted almost exclusively to dogs include *101 Dalmations* and *The Fox and the Hound.*

• Alfred Hitchcock made his traditional cameo appearance in his film *The Birds* accompanied by his two Sealyham Terriers and was so devoted to his dogs, he named his production company 'Shamley Productions', an anagram of Sealyham.

• Recent Hollywood canine blockbusters made in the 80s and 90s include *K9, Beethoven,* and *Turner and Hooch.*

Dogs in Advertising

• The dog 'Nipper', painted by his owner Francis Barraud in the late 19th century, is still used by the record company HMV to advertise their products.

• West Highland Terriers are now recognized worldwide since they were used to advertise a brand of Scotch whisky.

• The Old English Sheepdog has become so famous as a result of advertising paint, it is now popularly known as the 'Dulux' dog.

Outstanding Dogs

• The earliest dog skeleton was excavated at a site called Ein Mallaha in Israel and dates back about 12,000 years.
• The Romans used to equip their mastiffs with light armour and send them into battle against the enemy carrying spikes and cauldrons of flaming sulphur.
• The most famous Scottish dog, a Skye terrier known as 'Greyfriars Bobby', lived in the mid-1800s and earned his name in history by refusing to leave his master's grave until he himself died some ten years later.
• Sometime during the period 1820-24, a 'bull and terrier' dog named 'Billy' managed to attack and kill 4000 rats within 17 hours.

• The first dog to be sent into space in 1957 was a Russian dog named Laika.
• The tallest dog ever recorded was a Great Dane measuring 105.4cm (41.5ins) tall. The smallest, a Yorkshire Terrier, measured only 6.3cm (2.5ins) at the shoulder and 9.5cm (3.75ins) from head to tail.

Dog Names

If you're finding it difficult to find a name for your dog and 'Rover' or 'Sandy' simply don't appeal, you may be inspired by the following list of names which some of the most rich and famous people in history have bestowed upon their beloved canines.

Queen Alexandra	Basset Hound	*Babil*
Emily Brontë	Bullmastiff	*Keeper*
Richard Burton	Llasa Apso	*Georgia*
Prince Charles	Jack Russell Terrier	*Poor Pooh*
Agatha Christie	Manchester Terrier	*Treacle*
Winston Churchill	Poodle	*Rufus*
Charles Dickens	Mastiff	*Turk*
Walt Disney	Poodle	*Duchess*
Queen Elizabeth II	Welsh Corgi	*Dookie*
Sigmund Freud	Chow Chow	*Jo-Fi*
King George VI	Labrador Retriever	*Scrummy*
Thomas Hardy	Wire Fox Terrier	*Wessex*
Adolf Hitler	Scottish Terrier	*Negus*
John F Kennedy	German Shepherd	*Clipper*
Marilyn Monroe	Collie	*Muggsie*
Beatrix Potter	Pekingese	*Chuleh*
Franklin D. Roosevelt	Scottish Terrier	*Duffy*
Ringo Starr	Two Chow Chows	*Ying and Yang*
Elizabeth Taylor	Shih Tzu	*Mariposa*
Queen Victoria	Pomeranian	*Beppo*
William Wordsworth	Greyhound	*Dart*

Useful Addresses

Association of Pet
Behaviour Counsellors
257 Royal College Street
London NW1 9LU
Tel: 01386 751 151

Association of Pet Dog
Trainers
Maddox Lane
Bookham
Surrey
KT23 3HT
Tel: 01372 457854

The British Kennel Club
1 Clarges Street
Piccadilly
London W1Y 8AB
Tel: 0171 493 6651
Fax: 0171 495 6162

British Veterinary
Association
7 Mansfield Street
London W1M QAT
Tel: 0171 636 6541

Dogs Home Battersea
4 Battersea Park Road
London SW8 4AA
Tel: 0171 622 3626

Pedigree Petfoods
Education Centre
National Office
Waltham on the Wolds
Melton Mowbray
Leicester LE14 4RS
Tel: 0664 410000

Royal Society for the
Prevention of Cruelty to
Animals
Causeway
Horsham
West Sussex
RH12 1HG
Tel: 0403 64181

Glossary

Action: Movement, i.e. walking, trotting or running.

Amble: Relaxed easy movement in which legs on either side move in unison or almost as a pair.

Angulation: The angle at the joint where the bones meet.

Apron: Longer hair below neck on the chest. Frill.

Barrel: Rounded rib section.

Bat ear: An erect ear, broad at base, rounded at the top.

Bay: Prolonged sound of a hunting dog.

Beard: Thick, long hair on muzzle and underjaw.

Bitch: A female.

Blaze: White stripe running up centre of the face.

Blenheim: Chestnut and white markings.

Blue-merle: Blue and grey mixed with black. Marbled.

Bobtail: Naturally tail-less dog or one with tail docked very short.

Bolt: To drive an animal out of its earth or burrow.

Bowed: Curved outward.

Breed: Pure-bred dogs more or less uniform in size and structure.

Breed Standard: Description of ideal specimen in each breed.

Brindle: Even mixture of black hairs with lighter hairs, usually gold, brown or grey, and usually in stripes.

Brisket: Part of the body below the chest and between the forelegs.

Canines: The two upper and two lower long, sharp-pointed teeth next to the incisors.

Castrate: To remove the testicles of a male dog.

Chiselled: Clean cut, showing foreface bone structure.

Cobby: Short, compact body.

Crest: Upper, arched portion of the neck. Also the hair starting at stop on head and tapering off down neck.

Cropping: Trimming of the ear leather in order to make ear stand erect. Prohibited by the Kennel Club.

Crossbreed: A dog whose sire and dam are of two different breeds.

Dam: The female parent.

Dappled: Mottled marking of different colours.

Deadgrass: Straw to bracken colour.

Dewclaw: Fifth digit on the inside of the legs.

Dewlap: Loose, pendulous skin under the throat.

Dock: Amputation of the tail.

Domed: Evenly rounded skull shape.

Double coat: An outer weather-resistant coat, together with a warm and softer undercoat.

Drop ear: Ends of the ear folded or drooping forward.

Feathering: Long fringe of hair on ears, legs, tail or body.

Field trial: Competition for gundogs in which they are judged on ability and style in finding and/or retrieving game.

Flecked: Coat lightly ticked with another colour, but not spotted or roan.

Flews: Pendulous upper lips, particularly at the inner corners.

Flush: To drive birds from cover, to force them to take flight.

Foreface: The front part of the head, before the eyes. Muzzle.

Furrow: A slight indentation from stop to occiput.

Gait: Movement at various rates of speed, distinguished by a particular rhythm and stride.

Game: Hunted wild birds or animals.

Giving tongue: Barking or baying of hounds.

Gone to ground: When quarry has taken cover from hounds.

Grizzle: Mixture of colours including bluish-grey, red and black.

Hackney action: High lifting of the front feet.

Harefoot: An elongated foot like that of a hare.

Haunch: Buttock or rump.

Heat: Seasonal period of the female.

Hindquarters: Rear part of dog from loin.

Inbreeding: The mating of closely related dogs, such as father and daughter.

Interbreeding: The breeding together of dogs of different varieties of a breed.

Jowls: Flesh of lips and jaws.

Leather: Flap of the ear.

Mask: Dark shading on the foreface.

Merle: A colouration, usually blue-grey, with flecks of black.

Moult: Shedding of the coat.

Muzzle: The head in front of the eyes, nasal bone, nostrils and jaws.

Occiput: The highest, back point of skull.

Oestrus: The period during which a bitch becomes sexually active. (This may be over a week or two but she may only mate willingly for one or two days during oestrus.)

Pads: Tough, thickened skin on underside of the feet.

Pastern: Region of the foreleg between the wrist and the digits.

Pedigree: The written record of a dog's ancestry.

Pied: Unequally proportioned patches of white and another colour.

Plume: A long fringe of hair hanging from the tail.

Pointing: Freezing position on sight of game and pointing in its direction.

Prick ear: Carried erect and usually pointed at the tip.

Pure bred: A dog whose parents are of the same breed and are themselves of unmixed descent.

Range: To cover a wide area of ground.

Retrieve: The act of bringing back any article or game to the handler.

Roan: A fine mixture of coloured hairs alternating with white hairs.

Rose ear: A small drop ear which folds over and back.

Ruff: Thick, longer hair around the neck.

Runt: Weak, undersized puppy in the litter.

Sable: Coat colour. Black-tipped hairs against a background of gold, silver, grey, fawn or tan basic coat.

Scenthound: A dog which hunts by ground scent rather than sight.

Self colour: Whole colour except for lighter shadings.

Sighthound: A hound which courses game by sight rather than scent.

Spay: Surgical removal of the uterus and ovaries.

Stern: Tail of a sporting dog or hound.

Stop: The indentation between the eyes where the nasal bone and skull meet.

Stripping: The removal of old hair by hand from a wire-coated dog.

Topknot: Longer hair on top of head.

Trace: A black line extending from occiput to twist on a Pug.

Trail: To hunt by following ground scent.

Tricolour: Three-colour: black, white and tan.

Twist: Term used to describe a Pug's tail.

Well-sprung ribs: Ribs springing out from spinal column giving correct shape.

Whelps: Unweaned puppies.

Withers: The highest point of the body, immediately behind the neck.

Index

All photographs in this book were taken by B. Gibbs, Robert Smith, L. Hess, C. Seddon, Simon Everett, P.A. Broadbent and John W. Warren, and supplied courtesy of Natural Science Photographs, 33 Woodland Drive, Hertfordshire WD1 3BY, except: Pages 22, 29, 30, 31, 36, 37, 38, 39, 41, 42, 43, 45, 47, 48, 49, 51, 53, 74, 90, 150, 151, 153, 207, 218, 219, 220, 221, 223, 226, 227, 228, 229, Marc Henrie, ASC, 22 Warbeck Road, London W12; 237, *Noah's Ark*, Manuscript from Asturia, Spain, c. 950 (New York, Pierpont Morgan Library); 239, Bronze Chariot (British Museum, London); 241, *Parables of Our Lord*, by John Everett Millais (Routledge, 1864); 101 *Dalmations* © Walt Disney, 1996, provided courtesy of Walt Disney Company; 244, *Children of Charles I*, after Sir Anthony van Dyck, 1637 (National Portrait Gallery, London).